STRAIGHT
TO
NORMAL

Straight to Normal by Sharif D. Rangnekar is a heartfelt account of a gay man embracing his identity and sexuality in a society that ostracizes those who do not conform to bigoted notions of what is 'normal'. A powerful story of self-discovery and acceptance, this book is a celebration of one's individuality and the right that everyone should enjoy to live with dignity.
—Dr Shashi Tharoor

This book has filled a vacuum that existed in the age of Section 377. So often young gay people never thought it was possible to be in a loving, caring relationship. Nor was there a way to bridge the path to make society understand their reality. This can now happen.
—Anjali Gopalan, Founder, Naz Foundation

This is perhaps the first time that an autobiography of an Indian gay man, replete with closets, frustration, joy and celebration, has been published. Sharif Rangnekar, a well-known journalist, turns the gaze inward for his compelling narration. I feel proud that his courageous testimonial comes close at the heels of the landmark 377 judgement, offering readers a chance to understand how a heteronormative society can suffocate the 'other'.
—Apurva Asrani, scriptwriter of *Aligarh* and *Shahid*; national award-winning editor; and activist

This is a brave book, and anyone who is 'out' may recognize the struggles and joys Sharif describes. For those who are on their own journeys of coming out, Sharif's story may give courage and insight.
—Jon Miller, Founder, Open for Business

The personal is the political! This searing autobiography by Sharif is a must-read for anyone trying to understand what it means to have grown up queer under very challenging circumstances, and what freedom tastes like, at the end of it all. Our country needs more and more queer people to share their stories of triumph. We are here, we are queer and we aren't going away, darlings, so you better read this book to know more!
Parmesh Shahani, author of *Gay Bombay-Globalization, Love and (Be)longing in Contemporary India*

STRAIGHT TO NORMAL

MY LIFE AS A GAY MAN

SHARIF D. RANGNEKAR

RUPA

Published by
Rupa Publications India Pvt. Ltd 2019
7/16, Ansari Road, Daryaganj
New Delhi 110002

Sales Centres:
Allahabad Bengaluru Chennai
Hyderabad Jaipur Kathmandu
Kolkata Mumbai

Copyright © Sharif D. Rangnekar 2019

The views and opinions expressed in this book are the author's own and the facts are as reported by him which have been verified to the extent possible, and the publishers are not in any way liable for the same. Names of some people have been changed to protect their privacy.

All rights reserved.
No part of this publication may be reproduced, transmitted, or stored in a retrieval system, in any form or by any means, electronic, mechanical, photocopying, recording or otherwise, without the prior permission of the publisher.

ISBN: 978-93-5333-366-9

First impression 2019

10 9 8 7 6 5 4 3 2 1

The moral right of the author has been asserted.

Printed at Gopsons Papers Ltd, Noida

This book is sold subject to the condition that it shall not, by way of trade or otherwise, be lent, resold, hired out, or otherwise circulated, without the publisher's prior consent, in any form of binding or cover other than that in which it is published.

To all those souls who lost hope and life;
To all those queer,
living in the dark and out in the light;
to the activists who have worked tirelessly for our rights.

Preface

I am fifty years old and single. My story is similar to that of a large number of men who had to conform to a society that tried to suffocate gays behind its veneer. I want to live proudly in my country, but there have been times when I have also had the desire to leave it. Why leave without a fight, I often told myself, resisting the temptation of a more peaceful and accepting life, probably in Europe or Southeast Asia. I have been through depression, burnouts, highs and mellow periods. I have also experienced love, lust, anger, angst, anxiety, fear and even hate in equal measure.

On 6 September 2018, I got an alert on WhatsApp informing me that the Supreme Court had read down Section 377 and decriminalized homosexual sex, rendering an act that was 'unnatural' for centuries as 'natural'. It was a historic order, a triumph for the LGBTQ movement and a time to cherish as the order allowed people like me the freedom to express our sexuality without being afraid. Even though I had learnt to live in the fear of such hostility, I knew that my mother had always been terrified. She had been through many sleepless nights knowing that hate against people like me was a reality.

When the verdict reached me, I was away in a quiet and desolate area close to Cha Am in Thailand, a country where my sexuality is far more acceptable. With me was my close family, celebrating the order as an early birthday gift.

I narrated the many years of legal struggle, starting with the petition of 2001 by Naz Foundation, the 2009 Delhi High Court order and its reversal in 2013 by the Apex Court. I told them about the lives that had been lost, the suicides, the assaults, the rapes and police harassment of men like me. I revealed how activists were ostracized by society and hounded not just by the law but also by the media.

I thanked them for being a supportive family. I told them how lucky I was to speak freely about the community and myself. How liberating it was to be able to write songs on being gay, both in celebration and in protest against irrational ideas of morality imposed on us. How privileged I was that I could quit my job and become much more engaged with activist groups.

'Yes,' my brother said, 'but more important than having the law on your side, is for you to find someone special.' My brother wanted nothing more desperately than for me to find love and companionship.

I was close to tears but I held them back. It was not until the next morning when I was alone in the hotel room, reading messages, news reports and watching videos celebrating the verdict that I let myself go. I was close to hysterical. And, as clichéd as it may sound, my entire life flashed before my eyes.

Chapter One

I WAS THE third child in the family. After two sons, my father was hoping for a daughter but he got me—a slightly oversized baby boy. I was named Sharif after the Egyptian actor, Omar Sharif. My eldest brother, who was five years older, was named Dilip after the actor Dilip Kumar. My middle brother's name, Dwijen (or Duji as we preferred to call him) came from Dwijendra, who was a folk and classical singer from Bengal.

As is evident from our names, my parents loved music and films. We had a spool player with a collection of ghazals to Western music including recordings from Woodstock. My father, D.K. Rangnekar, was then the editor of *The Economic Times*. My mother, Veena, looked after the home and also explored her interests in designing clothes, painting and films. In the mid-1970s, she even became a member of the Censor Board of Film Certification (CBFC). Around the same time, she did a centre-spread for one of the leading women's magazines, modelling her self-designed and tailored outfits. Growing up, I was always fascinated by the clothes my mother designed.

As for Pa, spare time was about family and music. I remember how we celebrated the arrival of a record player in our home back in 1973 when I was just five years old. The record player pretty much pushed aside the spool player that was a bit cumbersome. My father had bought a pair of speakers and an amplifier as well. And, with it came the then popular film *Bobby*'s soundtrack LP.

I thought Rishi Kapoor was very handsome and would call him Rashi. I was almost obsessed by him and disliked anyone who praised Dimple Kapadia over my Rashi.

My father, who was born in Goa's Porvorim, was a brilliant student. His family moved from Goa to Mumbai where he did his college and later his PhD in economics from the London School of Economics. He had worked in London, Melbourne and Sri Lanka before returning to India.

Ma, a Kapoor, was a no-nonsense Punjabi kudi. While in school in Dehradun—the town they moved to from Lahore (where she was born) before Partition—Ma had even beaten up a couple of boys with her hockey stick and broken a few ribs because they had passed lewd comments at her.

For Ma and Pa, it was 'love at first sight'. Actually, it was my father's immediate decision to marry my mother, whom he had seen at a conference at Delhi's Vigyan Bhawan. He used all possible means to obtain Ma's family details and went to her parents with a marriage proposal. My mother was only nineteen years old then and was working at the city office of a European airline. She had not thought of marriage till then. Even though her parents were impressed by my father's credentials, the final decision was left to my mother. Ma kept Pa waiting for a couple of nights before she finally said yes.

My father had a large family. Even though his whole family attended his wedding and blessed him and Ma, the fact that Ma was a non-Maratha did not go down very well. With time, things settled down and Ma eventually became one of the favourites of my grandmother.

Pa, on the other hand, was welcomed and doted over by his in-laws in Delhi—the Kapoors. Our annual family vacation was always at their home. My father fell in love with the city, its wide spaces, the greenery and the fascinating monuments. This love for Delhi made him buy some land in the hope that he would retire and write a few books sitting in a home with a small patch of garden in the front.

Technically, Punjabi would qualify as my mother tongue but it was English that was spoken at home. Pa knew Marathi and a bit of Konkani besides English. Ma, however, spoke Hindi, English and a little Punjabi.

We lived on the sixth floor in Malabar Hill's Tenerife Apartments, just opposite the Atomic Energy building. We were amongst those few who did not own the flat we lived in. It was provided by the management of *The Economic Times*. Most of our neighbours either had businesses, links in the film industry, or were top-level executives attached to some of Mumbai's largest business houses.

In the public eye, my father was considered a futurologist, a leading economist and an editor who did not mind taking on the establishment of the day. He went on to be named amongst the top five hundred leaders of the world by *Time* magazine in 1977. All of this though, his achievements, only made sense to me when I was far older. At that time, I was just nine years old and my father was only my father.

Since Pa had worked his way up the ladder from a small town in Goa through academics and hard work, there was an unsaid expectation that the three of us, his sons, would do well at school and beyond. Our school was the tiny Bombay International School with under thirty students per class and no multiple sections.

In my class of around twenty-five students, we had an equal mix of boys and girls. I had just two close friends—Munna and Amit—and we often visited each other's homes. It was not unusual for either of them to stay over at my house on a weekend, playing board games and listening to music. Then, there was Sameer, whom I found attractive. He had short hair, slightly dark skin, thin, almost bony, with a cut on his left eyebrow. He had a warm smile, was soft-spoken and very polite. I don't know what it was about him but I found his whole demeanour beautiful. However, I barely spoke to him.

I also spent a lot of my time with my brothers' friends, joining them for cricket, kabaddi, kick the can, and robbers and thieves. Being the youngest, I was always following my brothers, trying to be on their team in any game.

In one instance though, I got placed in the opposite team and both of them on the other one. Not being agile, I failed to stop the ball, letting it cross the boundary and an angry captain of the team, called me a sissy. When I failed to stop the ball again, he came and pulled down my shorts in the middle of the playground of the Atomic Energy building, something that had never happened before when I had misfielded playing in the team either of my brothers were in. I remember pulling up my shorts and running away amidst loud laughter. I also remember that my brothers just stood there and watched. This incident took a harsh turn as my father scolded them for not preventing my humiliation.

I was not the most peaceful child though, especially at home. Maybe because I was the most pampered among the three boys, I just had to have things my way. I would throw things around if my demands weren't met. The reason for my outbursts could be anything—the taste of the food served to me, the music I wanted to listen to or my brothers ignoring me particularly when they planned to go out with friends. I went off the handle if they monopolized the washroom, getting ready to impress some girl or the other.

I was particular about the way I looked at social gatherings and needed time to dress, I never found any girl attractive, I was indifferent towards them. I had just a couple of boys as friends, whereas my brothers had a large group of friends including 'favourite' girls. As for me, my only 'favourite' was Sameer, the person I had no courage to speak to.

School was never stressful, at least not at that stage. We had no homework, tuitions were unheard of and extra-curricular activities were strongly encouraged. But what I enjoyed most was the music class. Almost every report card said I was most attentive and happy during the music class.

I was ten years old when Pa decided to quit *The Economic Times* to move to *Business Standard* as its editor. This meant we had to move to Kolkata, the headquarters of that newspaper. I did not know what to expect. All I knew then was that we would have to clear some entrance exams and were hopeful of being admitted to St Xavier's School.

Chapter Two

WE REACHED KOLKATA in the middle of January 1979. We had no idea about this city, no preconceived notions. We only knew that it was the capital of West Bengal, dominated by Bengalis and that Hindi was hardly spoken. Another thing we found out soon enough—unlike Bombay, this city experienced winters.

The slightly cooler temperature was immediately felt as we got off the train at the Howrah station, but, the hustle bustle at the station, the chaos of coolies and the sheer noise that prevailed around us made us forget everything else. We drove out of the station, and with each traffic signal, we could see the gigantic Howrah Bridge appear less distant. As we moved ahead, the 'wow' factor of the bridge was somewhat lost amidst the potholes, the mix of vehicles and the bumpy ride of lane-less driving. This muddle of things reminded us of Crawford Market which also thrived on chaos. Kolkata seemed to be exactly that, at least for the first half of our drive towards the centre of the city.

First, we checked in to the Grand Hotel on Chowringhee for four nights after which we were to move to New Kenilworth Hotel before settling into our home at New Alipore that was going to be ready in the next three to four weeks, or so we were told. Ultimately, for three long months, we lived out of suitcases and ate hotel food with the occasional rice and dal, which was offered only when our guts collapsed one by one. We had heard that the water in the city had a way of upsetting the stomach. This also explained why just about every street had a pharmacy.

Being in a hotel had its initial novelty and a sense of being served while doing nothing. But the novelty lost its sheen pretty quickly as we missed having our own kitchen along with a living room and bedrooms. In fact, we longed for the whole idea of the structured existence that a home gave.

There was, at best, a locational advantage that the hotel offered. We were just minutes away from Park Street—the most upmarket part of the city with restaurants, bars and outlets with live music. We weren't far from the famous New Market either. And our school, St Xavier's, was only a few streets away.

By April that year, we were in our new home. For the first time, we were living in a bungalow. It was a corner house with a front lawn, large verandah and a cute little kitchen garden on the side. There were three bedrooms with two of the larger ones being separated only by a door. These two rooms became the master bedrooms: one for my parents and the other shared by my brothers. The third room was reserved as a study-cum-guest room. Although I had a bed to sleep in my brothers' room as well, I slept in my parents' room on a mattress on the floor adjacent to their bed. At times, I even slipped in-between my parents in their bed.

The first few months at school were difficult, as my stomach did not hold up. All the going in and out of hospital made my lack of attendance a matter of concern for the school authorities. However, had I been well, I doubt I would have been happy going to school in any case. I think I missed the familiarity of my batch and the intimacy of the small classes we used to have in Bombay International School, where there were less than four hundred students and parents knew other parents as well as teachers.

I made almost no friends in my first year, failing that class due to poor attendance. My health overshadowed what was indeed a dismal performance in the few exams I had given. I was certain that Pa, given his qualifications and stature as an economist, would be upset, but he never said much, except that it would take time to adjust to the new city and its people.

But, nothing really changed.

Although I passed class five in my second attempt—that is one whole year wasted—I struggled in class six as well, being held back a year yet again with a combination of repeated gastro problems and, what my principal and class teacher claimed, a lack of attention and interest. I remember Pa asking my class teacher if there was a way of overcoming these so-called hurdles, a way that would help me become more attentive and interested.

There was no other answer except the oft-repeated need to focus on studying, mugging up and passing papers.

'He doesn't communicate with me, his other teachers or anyone else.' My class teacher seemed to be trying to point to something concrete, whatever that might be.

As I repeated class six, the attention from my new class teacher, Ronald Gass (a charismatic and handsome man who was very popular across the school for his smart and athletic looks) started to make a difference to my confidence and application. He was strict, but very kind. He would sit and guide me through different subjects, check on my health, discuss music and food with me and even slip in odd bits of trivia on the books I should read. He had also put me in charge of the class on different occasions, giving me the key to the only and all-important cupboard we had in our classroom.

He spoke well about me to Pa and Ma, only reminding them that the teachers of some subjects felt I talked too much in class and was distracted easily. His other concern was my roly-poly figure–something that I saw as a huge benefit. The increasing weight and waist size made me a bully. I would routinely punch out the boys who kept reminding me that I had failed twice or those who mocked my size.

Fortunately, there were some classmates who never commented

on my past, or my present, and we slowly became friends. They began coming to my home at times to play cricket in the lawn or to enjoy the food Ma made—the famous chaat of Delhi and pav bhaji of Bombay.

I would have liked to call so many others, boys who had pretty faces, friendly warm smiles and lithe bodies, like Sameer in Bombay. I, somehow, never managed to reach out to them or make any of them my friend.

At home, there was a calmness since now I was more in tune with school and the city although I would overhear conversations that maybe I needed some kind of physical activity as I continued to put on weight. While many called me a bully at school, at home I still showed the same streaks of anger, admittedly less frequently than I had in Bombay. I knew that if I could pin my brothers down, I would not even need to fight them. All I had to do was just sit on them and I would emerge victorious.

They, as had been the case in Bombay, had a large set of friends, including people in New Alipore. They hung out with them and had them over. On Sundays, they, with their friends, took an early morning tram to head to China Town for breakfast and, once in a while, also made it to a disco in central Kolkata. Their social life and activities grew as they both moved into St James' School, which was known for extra-curricular activities like the arts including music and theatre.

It was at the same time that I moved to class seven and was now without either of my brothers in the same school. I was also unhappy to find a largely unfamiliar set of classmates as the school had decided to shuffle us around into different sections. I was, once again, compelled to build new bonds and recreate a group. It was tedious and I missed Mr Gass and the way he had taught us.

I did, however, find a new friend in Aman—a boy with straight, short hair, big eyes and body language that for some reason seemed feminine. Even his intonation was similar to women's. He was a lot like two seniors in our school—famously called pansies—who appeared to be very close friends as they walked the corridors huddled close together.

Aman, because of his so-called lady-like movements, was an easy target for bullying. He was called names like 'sissy' and 'pansy' and some Bengali words that I did not understand. Some even taunted him about his lack of manliness questioning 'how much of a man was he'. Aman, was least bothered, holding his handkerchief like a girl, he waved each comment or question away in a dismissive manner. He continued to speak and behave just the way he had on the first day I had seen him in class. His hand movements were exaggerated and his joy was always loud. Sometimes, especially when he had got good news, one could see him skipping like a girl.

I was in touch with some of my old friends from class six who were now in different sections and most of them did not like Aman. If he was there, they would tease him so much, beating him to the ground, reducing him to tears. I did try to stop them, maybe just once or twice, but with no real assertiveness as I did not want to be outside of that 'pack' because of defending Aman.

I realized that the only way to avoid such skirmishes was to meet him separately, without the rest of the gang. He also seemed to like that, particularly the attention he got from Ma. Even Pa would chat with him, occasionally joking in an affectionate way.

'That is lipstick, isn't it?' Pa had asked him when he had noticed his red-coloured lips. Aman nodded his head, looking slightly frightened.

'Just like a little lady,' my father commented, tickling him. Aman had smiled with a lot of delight.

Aman was interested in all that I did, be it the music I listened to, the food I liked or the walks I took in the area close to our home. He never once commented on my obese body or why I had failed in the past.

'I don't care what people say about me. I am the way I am,'

he had told me, while cantering down the street.

Even as I had got this new friend, the best one I would like to think, my marks in school kept dipping. My interest levels were plummeting. I was struggling in Bengali, Hindi and history. The stomach bug came back to haunt me as well. I barely crossed the line and passed. My parents who were very concerned felt I was missing a co-ed school and needed to be closer to home as I was alone at St Xavier's. This made them consider St Paul's School which was situated a few kilometres away in the Kidderpore area.

Thus, after a short break in the month of March 1984, I entered a new school in class eight. It was a smaller school than St Xavier's but still a lot larger than Bombay International School. We had a very short session of a few weeks as the school was to break for summer earlier than normal.

In this short period of my new school life, I got to know a few boys. One of them was much larger than me, and I was relieved as I was not the fattest one any more. I was asked many times why I had left St Xavier's as that was the school many of them had hoped to be a part of. I told them that my parents felt I should be in a co-educational system rather than in an all-boys school. Their immediate assumption was that I fancied girls and was longing to have a girlfriend—a thought I never had.

One day, soon after my Hindi tuitions that I had started a few days earlier, I seemed to hit a sudden period of unhappiness. Till date, I have no idea why it happened or what was going through my mind. But that afternoon as I sat at my desk at home, I took out the pointed divider from my Camlin pencil case and used the sharp tip to write—'I do not wish to live. Life is not good', on the desk.

Then, I got up, picked up a bottle of mercurochrome that lay in the medicine chest in the dining room. I knew it was poison. I took it to the toilet and stared at it. Slowly, I removed the cap of the bottle with the intent to drink all the contents.

'*Maybe everyone will miss me or maybe they would not miss me at all!*' I vaguely remember these thoughts running through my mind.

I spent a couple of minutes doing nothing, just sitting on the cover of the Western-style commode with the open bottle in my hand. Finally, I replaced the cap and put the bottle down. I got goosebumps just thinking what I had almost done.

I placed the bottle of mercurochrome back in the medicine chest and returned to my desk. This time, I took out an ink bottle, unscrewed the cap and poured out the contents over the partially-etched writing, hoping the dark blue of the ink would hide whatever was there so no one would see the sentences ever. I scraped off the wood too, so that any semblance of recognizable words was erased.

I struggled to sleep that night.

Chapter Three

THE SUMMER HOLIDAYS were soon upon us. It was that time of the year that Pa took us on our annual vacation. After moving from Mumbai, the holidays were more often to places such as Trivandrum, Digha, Goa or even to Mumbai. Our visits to Delhi had reduced as Ma's brother and family had moved to Mumbai.

However, this year, there was no plan at all. In the third week of April, before our schools broke for our long holidays, there was a strike at the offices of the Anandabazar Patrika Group (ABP Group), the owners of *Business Standard*. The strike, which was called a 'lockout', resulted in the press machinery coming to an absolute halt. This meant there were no newspapers or journals being published from the ABP Group.

Pa and his colleagues were not allowed into their offices; they were not even allowed to enter the building. At times the threat of violence was such that even being seen on the road that led to his workplace was considered dangerous. It was a situation that Pa had never experienced. I remember him telling us that his stint in Australia setting up a research bureau had been smooth. His period with a local and powerful newspaper in Ceylon had also been largely good barring the fact that the powers in charge of the island nation wanted him out. Being a foreigner, they felt his scoops were motivated and not in the interest of their nation. Even with *The Economic Times*, there was a long run with the exception of differences of opinion with the management. 'Such differences were not unusual,' he had told us.

But a lockout and a strike by the union, which he said was more to do with local politics, was something else entirely. Ma asked us not to pressurize him about taking a holiday as he was already very tense. He was used to commenting on the state of the nation and its politics and writing editorials. Thus, withholding information and views, and sitting at home was against his grain and the aggression on the ground along with the uncertainty of when there would be a settlement was 'something different and difficult' which we would probably not even understand, said Ma.

The circumstances, however, made sure we saw Pa every day that summer. What never changed though were his morning and evening calls, checking up on the news and the union situation at the ABP Group.

As the strike and its uncertainties settled into Pa's mind, he was a bit more relaxed, taking us out to the Tollygunge Club on several occasions. He even took Dilip to a bar and got him his first drink—a whiskey. He allowed him to drive but controlled the speed to as little as twenty-five km per hour.

The whole of May and most of June went like this and none of us were regretting that our holidays were being spent in Kolkata.

By around the third week of June, the lockout was lifted, although the union situation had not been resolved. Pa could enter office and he slowly started resuming the daily publication of *Business Standard*. Ma was relieved because this whole long period, which was very happy for us as a family, had taken a toll on Pa.

On 29 June, Pa returned early from office saying he was not feeling well. He had a mild fever and lay in bed all afternoon and evening. He had a light dinner and slept off again. That night, as usual, I was in my parents' room. It was past 1 a.m. when Pa woke up. He was struggling to open the toilet door. I helped him and as we managed to open the door, he threw up. He looked completely worn out, finding it difficult to even walk back to bed.

As I helped him, Ma woke up.

His feet were cold, his face looked pale and he started asking for the 'boys' while looking fondly at Ma. I went and woke up Dilip and Duji. We were all in that room when Pa looked at all us, one by one, before heaving a sigh and leaving us. It was a massive cardiac arrest, we were told later. Ma remained silent for hours in shock, almost through the whole night until her mother—our grandmother, who we called Mom—arrived from Mumbai. She shook her out of her shock and made her cry.

Dilip cried too but he tried to console Duji and me. I even fought with the doctor, who we had called in to check on Pa, saying that his declaration that my father had passed away was not true. I pointed to Pa's still-ticking watch, assuming naively that the watch only worked on a live pulse.

By early morning, our home was teeming with people from his office as well as the Sarkars' who owned the ABP Group. Family started to arrive soon after, from Delhi and Mumbai. The next day, local and national newspapers published about Pa's demise on their front pages.

As the crowds left and the condolences continued over telex, letters, phone calls and visits, we were more or less down to ourselves and Ma. It was decided that we would move to Delhi. This was the most feasible option as we had no other home and Ma's sister and her family was there to help us through the Delhi system.

At a time when everything seemed to look bleak and uncertain, we latched on to every possible positive. I remember Ma saying we were extremely fortunate that the last instalment of the loan on the Delhi two-storey bungalow that Pa had built, had just been paid. Three months earlier, the previous lease that was for both the floors, had lapsed, almost timed in a divine manner ensuring we had a floor to ourselves. As a family, we also felt that the strike at the ABP Group was something of a divine intervention as it gave us almost two months with Pa at home with us, bringing us closer to each other than ever before.

All through this ordeal, our mother was a pillar of strength for us. It was only many years later that Ma told us that she was just going through the motions. She was completely ignorant of public life, banking, money matters and budgets. Ma even acknowledged she did not even know how to write a cheque. The first cheque she wrote was crossed, marked bearer and self—all in one!

Our biggest concern as a family though was Delhi's reputation of being an unsafe city. We used to read murders and assaults regularly in newspapers and feared living there. How would it be without Pa in a city such as Delhi—this was a question that came to Duji and me, weeks after Pa had passed away and we were packing to move.

Ma was now all we had. We never saw her cry or get angry during that period. Her colourful outfits were put away, turning every day into whites and greys. It was only a few years ago that I was made aware of the fact that she was told to follow this ritual as a reminder that she was now a widow and her colourful past had been with Pa who was no longer with her.

She was just forty-three years old then.

Chapter Four

I WAS THE first to reach Delhi, several weeks ahead of the rest, since every day of absence from my new school—Frank Anthony Public School (FAPS)—could have gone against me. So, there I was without my family, but with recognizable relatives, many parks and residential complexes and a population that spoke predominantly in Hindi, completely disregarding the fact that I wasn't fluent in the language. I remember hearing comments that suggested I was a snob because why else would I speak in English?

My first home in this city was my Uma masi's house. Residing in East of Kailash's C Block, my masi's was a closely knit family where everyone shared the household responsibilities, something which I loved and admired. In fact, I would also step in occasionally, baking a cake or just helping Masi with chores I was used to doing around the house.

She was a lecturer of English at Lady Shri Ram College and her husband, Bir uncle, was a lawyer who was privileged to have a chamber at the Delhi High Court. Like at our home, here too, art mattered. Masi was a painter, in her own right, and did a series of oils of peacocks and rooftops of old towns she had visited. Bir uncle, on the other hand, loved ghazals and spoke fluent Urdu. This also explained why my cousins—Mehtab and Aftab—had the names they did. His passion for Urdu poetry literally pushed Mehtab into singing and Aftab into playing the tabla. He himself was proficient in playing the harmonium and thus, among the three of them, they could easily pull off an evening of poetry and songs. Though at that time, my cousins did not like the pressure and compulsions of meeting the desires of their father, now neither of them regret it.

Another reflection of their interest in arts and literature was the mountains of books in the many shelves of their two-bedroom home. Masi also had a number of respected writers amongst her friends. She possessed a love for plays as well and attended whatever little theatre was available at that time.

My first few weeks at school were far from smooth. It was not just about the language barrier as everyone spoke Hindi during recess, it was the questions I was asked every few days by someone or the other. The ones that always got me into tears were 'who is your father' and 'what does he do'. There were times when my family was even accused of being British or not Indian enough just because I told them that we spoke English at home. The fact that my Uma masi taught literature at LSR also did not help my case as they went on to find another 'fault', questioning my first name and its Arabic lineage, doubting whether I was Hindu or Indian. 'No wonder you don't speak Hindi,' some of them would say, implying it was the universal language of the country.

I would run off to the infirmary in tears, spending hours with the warm and friendly nurse, Ms Kennedy. She would listen to me calmly, make suggestions and would often say that time heals everything. 'It is Delhi and its culture which is different from both the cities you have lived in,' she said, adding that once my mother and brothers would arrive, I would be more at home.

Her assessments were accurate.

Once Ma, Dilip and Duji arrived, we were soon shifting to our own home in Gulmohar Park. Our two-storey bungalow had a front lawn, a backyard and a driveway with a garage. There was a servants' quarters too. Our tenants on the ground floor were a small family from the advertising world with links in Mumbai. They welcomed us as though the home was theirs and we were guests, making us very comfortable, helping us settle in.

Our first floor home had two bedrooms and a long living-cum-dining with open terraces on either side. There was no staircase to reach the rooftop terrace, except by climbing a bamboo ladder. I was quite frightened of climbing up as the gap between the top rung of the ladder and the terrace was a lot more than three steps; Ma and Dilip could scale it with ease.

Our first 'settled' day at home happened to be my birthday. It was the day that Ma indulged me. She bought a two-in-one cassette and radio system along with detachable speakers, arranged a cake and cooked a special kind of mutton along with the regular rice, dal, vegetables and chapatti.

In the days to come, I started to get comfortable with my routine. I was at ease taking the bus to school every morning, making friends in class, doing my homework in the evenings, and helping Ma at home. It wasn't that I had suddenly taken to studying or started enjoying any specific subject in class as such, but I also was not as troubled as before about the culture at school.

As luck would have it, the then prime minister, Indira Gandhi, was assassinated on the morning of 31 October. None of us in class could make sense of the calamity that had befallen us or its political ramifications; all we knew was that she was a respected leader. We were rushed home a little earlier than normal, clueless about what was yet to unfold.

While the nation went into mourning, the anti-Sikh riots broke out. We were all frightened. We could hear bellows of fire down the street as some taxi stand had been torched. Some even claimed that the colony behind us was a threat as it was dominated by Sikhs. While we never experienced any untoward incident in our colony, we did hear of stories from other parts of the city including the close-by AIIMS complex. There were news reports saying over two thousand had been killed across the country and most of them just in Delhi.

Finally, though peace prevailed, the calm was uneasy. We were slowly getting back to what life was like before but Ma, for some reason, was not keeping well. She had a few days of nausea accompanied by mild fever and weakness. Given the state of the city, we had not given her health a serious thought. But now could not postpone it and took her for a check-up. Doctors suggested a certain surgery. The whole family was torn between the emotional state of Ma vis-à-vis the medical advice. It was the latter that prevailed leading to her being hospitalized in a large nursing home in Kailash Colony.

A whole system was put in place with Mom—our grandmother in charge to ensure that I would visit ma on some days and head directly back home from school on others. Uma masi was also involved, arranging food and sitting beside Ma when she was recovering. Since Dilip and Duji were at college, reaching home towards the evening on most days, the schedules of Mom and Uma masi revolved around my timings with the objective that I was never alone at our residence.

However, one fine day, I received the keys to our home with the expectation that I would be cautious, careful and safe, eating whatever food had been kept for me and that my homework, if any, would be completed. I had never been left alone at home,— not in Mumbai or in Kolkata or even at Uma masi's house during my initial stay in Delhi.

On that day, being the only one at home, I could do anything I wanted. I could throw my shoes wherever I wished to, dump my socks wherever I took them off. I could remain in my school uniform! Most importantly, I could lie with my feet up on our three-seater sofa—a definite no-no for any of us. I could also pick up any VHS and watch a video with no control over the length of time because no one was supposed to return until 4.30–5 in the evening. And it was just 2 p.m.

I rummaged through a few of the video cassettes we had and saw one marked 'Hot Tracks'. It was the only music programme, I think, that was available on Doordarshan during those days. As it came late on Friday nights (and we had school on Saturdays), I was only allowed to watch it later, if recorded.

I put down my plate in which a few morsels of rice and dal were still left. I turned on the video, lay on my side so that I could see the TV screen comfortably and started to watch some of the songs that were popular then. I forwarded a few of them but enjoyed watching others like 'You Might Think' by The Cars and 'Time After Time' by Cyndi Lauper. I was forwarding one of the songs when I suddenly saw a video of a black artist. It was Jermaine Jackson and the song was the popular dance track, 'Dynamite'.

The video was set in a jail and Jermaine—who looked a lot like his famous brother, Michael—was in an orangey-red sleeveless shirt and pants. He was supposed to be a convict trying to escape with a bunch of other men. Each one of them was fit and muscular to the extent that was pleasing to the eye and did not look overtly like bodybuilders. Their bodies shimmered and shone every time light fell on them. They had taut chests, slim frames and were moving gracefully, running, dancing, jumping over tables and dodging the jail security.

As I remained glued and fixated on the screen, I realized a sense of excitement taking over me. My hand had, subconsciously, unzipped my white school shorts and slipped in through the open fly to experience something I never had before. To my surprise, I had a boner—a word I learnt a few decades later. I could not stop myself as my hand, in that position, was giving me a feeling of delight or ecstasy or a happiness that was unusual. I could feel some kind of electricity or energy running through me.

Those few minutes of bliss did end eventually. However, I had not realized when the song had got over and another one had begun. None of what was playing through the video mattered any more. I was tired. My hands were sticky. I did not know what to do. I did not even know what had happened. I just lay there for a few minutes, not moving at all, staring at the ceiling, leaving my hand where it was, my heart beating faster and louder than normal. 'What was this?' I wondered.

Even as the search for an answer was imperative, the experience was something I wished to repeat and enjoy. I did exactly that, playing the video again the next afternoon, with a similar glee rising in my chest resulting from my own physical excitement. Tired as I was after this 'exercise', I continued to lie on the sofa as I had earlier, staring at the ceiling, but this time I was feeling a sense of guilt. Were my acts good or bad? Was it healthy or a risk?

The fear of not knowing finally led me to search for a book—any book—that would have something to do with sex. I remembered, as a younger boy, I had overheard my brothers talking about semen as a sticky white substance and 'wanking off', whatever that meant. 'Was it semen that I had released,' I asked myself.

Then, I remembered seeing a book with a silhouette of a man beside a woman. I had seen it on one of the shelves at home. It had been made clear to me that it was meant for adults, so I never had the courage to pick it up, especially not when everyone was at home. Now, though, I had those occasional few hours alone before Ma returned from the nursing home, I decided to find it and skim through the pages.

I went through shelf after shelf, row after row and after what felt like hours, I finally spotted it. It was called *The Naked Ape* by Desmond Morris. The blurb on the back claimed that it was the study of man, 'his sexual and social habits, his aggressions and affections'. I went through several pages and found something that suggested that when the 'species', that is man, cannot find sexual interaction, it usually finds its own means which is called masturbation. I read more and drew a parallel between my circumstances and what was written in the book. I understood that what I had been doing was normal and not unusual, nor was it unhealthy.

I was relieved and placed the book back in the spot where I could find it easily, if required again.

My habit to masturbate did not end there. Now with my Ma home, and my grandmother, too, there was no space or privacy for me to 'indulge', thus leaving the toilet as the only option. I let my imagination run, conjuring up images of Jermaine Jackson and some of the other men from the video, allowing myself that little elation.

Chapter Five

DELHI WAS FINALLY seeping into our lives as we got a sense of permanence at our home. I think we had resigned to the fact that this was where we were going to pitch tent forever. I am not sure whether it was the mundane routine or our growing familiarity with the city which helped us feel more settled, overcoming the loss we had experienced along with the change in location.

We did have our happy memories of Mumbai and remembered Pa often, many a time over a meal as he loved food. I think sometimes he was the reason we cooked a certain meat dish or put a special tadka on our dal... just because he loved it like that. The fact remained that we missed him, a lot. I remember all of us were in tears on his first death anniversary in 1985. We cried less in the coming years but we continued with the practice of organizing a havan for the next three decades as it was a ritual we felt we must do.

We thanked our stars and his long-sighted wisdom for the home we lived in and the education we received. Given that none of us was earning a penny even then, whatever funds we had were a result of his hard work—as Ma kept reminding us often.

I never asked Ma then or even later how she felt during that time but I saw gradual changes in her personality. Towards the beginning of 1985, Mom told her to put away her whites and greys and let the colour return to her life. She encouraged her to paint once again. The support from her mother possibly led her to put up a series of faces and nudes—all charcoal pieces of arts on canvas—that she had sketched years ago. She even occasionally wore a sleeveless top or a dress just like she had when Pa was there.

However, this return to art and herself was taken away as soon as it had re-entered her life, apparently due to comments from people close to us. How could a widow display such liberation—hindsight, I suspect this rhetoric stole some of who she was. A few years ago I did ask Ma specifically why this had happened. She only said that Delhi was a different city back then and added softly, 'I think it still is.' She almost inferred that her relationship and marriage to Pa had been far more liberating.

Ma never allowed anything to come in the way of being our mother and friend, particularly to my brothers who were older and required less care and protection (as parents would put it) than me. As a result, even without Pa, there was a kind of certainty and normalcy to our lives. My brothers continued to have a growing set of friends from within the colony and college. They even travelled out over the weekends to Jaipur, Meerut and Agra. Ma looked after home and simultaneously attended a course on child development at the National Institute of Public Cooperation and Child Development (NIPCCID). Later, she even started studying naturopathy and acupressure.

I, on the other hand, was in class nine by then; I was someone who hung on to the routine of home to school and school to home with the occasional diversion to meet the extended family at Uma masi's house. I was yet to explore Gulmohar Park and had no friends, either at school or at home.

I remember a close friend and a poet who visited Ma often said that I was a recluse—it was a word that held no meaning for me until I found it in a dictionary legitimizing who I was. One of my aunts also felt that I needed to grow up a bit faster. 'Sharif is still to find his feet it seems, he isn't interacting enough and not growing up,' I had overheard her saying once.

I was confused because I thought I was growing up. In fact, to many I was becoming a man. I had a slight moustache, there were hair growing on my arms and legs, which was a sign of manliness, just like my brothers and their friends. All of them were hairy and sporting beards, but soon they shaved them off opting for the clean-shaven look as made trendy by our new prime minister of the time, Rajiv Gandhi. For me, shaving was gratifying for its results but was a tedious affair. As for the growing hair on my arms and legs, it was an ugly sight and there was no way to get rid of them.

Dilip and Duji's short breaks out of Delhi became a regular affair, what with college festivals and their ability to be a part of a group that took such trips with utmost ease. Even I felt I wanted to go out somewhere, anywhere. But when I asked Ma to accompany me, she refused saying she wanted to stay in Delhi, look after home and continue the classes she was attending.

So, she made arrangements for me—a short trip to Kolkata. Consulting her sisters, including her cousins, it was decided that I could stay with Latika (the daughter of my Sheila masi), who was to visit Kolkata. As it turned out, Latika would have some company, me—a person who was familiar with the city—and I would be in safe hands with someone older, a reassurance for Ma.

Returning to Kolkata was a far more pleasant experience than when we had lived there or when we were leaving it. The memories of my schooldays and of losing Pa were still very fresh though. But, that October, I had a sense of peace at being left alone. I explored New Market, Victoria Memorial and Park Street, without having to report back to anyone. I ventured down to Free School Street and hopped across to Kathleens to eat a chicken patty or headed to a kathi roll place gobbling up a large number of rolls. I even took Latika to all of these places but most of all I enjoyed roaming around the city much like a solo traveller.

On one such occasion when I was unaccompanied, I stood and watched the buzz of men and women walking around New Market. I was standing beside a kebab and kathi roll shop called

Karco when my eyes fell on a small-framed, slightly frail young boy in a sleeveless T-shirt and tight shorts. I think he was a local Chinese, probably from the China Town area of the city. He might have been my age or maybe slightly older. It was hard to fathom. My eyes quickly moved from his face towards his waist and then remained glued to the crotch of the shorts he wore, noticing a slight bulge. I might have been staring at him for over a minute or more, not realizing how fixed my stare was. Everything else had blurred.

I got out of that trance only when he moved towards me, smiled and brushed his hands against my groin. There was something mischievous in his eyes. Even though I was surprised, I did not mind the brushing of his hand at all. He had touched the most private part of my body which was responding with the same excitement that I had experienced while watching the Jermaine Jackson video.

As I looked back to see him walk away, I noticed his very clean arms and legs that had no semblance of hair. He did not have a moustache either. He looked so smooth and reminded me of the character Chang from *Tintin in Tibet*, someone I had occasionally dreamt of. My dreams were ambitious enough to replace Tintin with myself, the saviour of Chang, holding him tightly in my arms, pulling him out of a cave in the Himalayas—just as the original story went.

That moment was thrilling and mixed with the independence of being alone in Kolkata, it turned my day into an adventure.

Within minutes, I bought a new razor—as I was carrying none—with the intention of shaving my growing moustache. There was a tiny stubble on my chin too which I felt was far from attractive, not that I was anything to look at, weighing over ninety kg then.

As I walked out of the store, I noticed a display of Anne French hair remover in different colours and fragrances. It was a popular hair removing lotion that many women used that time. 'Maybe I could go back to my room and quietly remove all the hair from my arms, legs and thighs,' I thought on an impulse, yet I was hesitant knowing that the lotions were not for men.

I stepped out of the store wondering how the storekeeper would react if I asked to buy that product. I don't know where I got the confidence from, but I walked right back inside and asked if they had such a product as my sister wanted one. I, in my bravado, pretended to not have seen any, even though there was a display large enough to trip me over. 'Which is the most popular fragrance?' I asked, continuing my pretence, picking up whatever he suggested, which was a sandalwood fragrance lotion.

After making the purchase, I rushed back to my hotel room, closed the door, locked it and almost tore open the packaging. There were some instructions in the box, the lotion and a miniature spatula. Fearing I might break into rashes, I applied the lotion on the upper arm, let it soak in for a bit before removing it with some cotton. The skin did feel slightly warm and the smell was nothing worth inhaling, but there was no adverse reaction. So, I applied the lotion on the rest of my arms, legs and thighs, and followed the instructions.

Soon, I had beautiful arms and legs, which were soft to touch. My hands moved across these parts of my body again and again not believing how simple it was to get petal-soft skin.

It was dinner time by then and Latika would be waiting for me. As I walked down the stairs to the dining area, I felt exposed as if there was a kind of nakedness about me for everyone to see. I wondered whether Latika would notice that I no longer had hair on my arms and legs.

I started to retrace my steps when one of the attendants called out to me that my cousin was waiting for me at a corner table at the lobby-level restaurant. I hoped that the mildly lit corner and my hurried walk would blur the details of the lost hair. It was a nervous dinner and every time I stretched my arms out to pass a dish, I feared she would notice the change and say something. Fortunately, she did not!

Chapter Six

I WAS BACK in Delhi after my week-long vacation. Ma was waiting for me at the station. It was a family tradition to pick up and drop off any of us who was travelling by air or train. Ma did it when Pa was around and continued that tradition for years to come. It didn't matter whether it was Dilip, Duji or I, she would always be there to receive us. It was something I habitually followed when I grew up.

As we walked towards the parking lot, I wondered if Ma noticed my hairless arms and legs. But she didn't seem to observe that difference, only saying there was a new spring in my gait. 'This holiday seems to have done you some good!' she said, making an observation, unaware of how adventurous I had actually been. Her assumption though was not completely inaccurate as I had become slightly more sure of things, although not knowing what I was sure about.. It was probably an upped confidence level, who knows.

Holidays were over and it was school as usual. I had begun to enjoy conversations with my class teacher—Rupi as we called him. He was a slim, young—just about thirty years old—sardar. He was an athlete, enjoyed music and seemed to have a sense of who we were as students and what each one of us liked. He would sit with us during breaks or even in class, asking us specific things such as what did we do on a Sunday, what we liked, which kind of food we ate, what was in our tiffins, and did not even mind quipping and cracking a joke with us. He was our buddy of sorts.

I think I was not the only one who enjoyed having him as our class teacher. He made studying more easy and fun. He took away the pressure and instead nudged us to focus not only on the books and pages we were supposed to read and learn from, but on ourselves. As a result, class nine passed off without any unpleasant incident. I had over 70 per cent as an average in all subjects, and I cruised into class ten.

As a family, we seemed to be sculpting our characters and defining our lives and habits. My second brother, Duji, liked to shut the door of the room that he shared with Dilip, especially when he was studying. He got irritated even if we knocked at the room door to ask if he wanted tea or to inform him that lunch or dinner was laid. He was the methodical one, bringing order to anything he did, even if it was sharing responsibilities in the kitchen, allocating what each one of us would do. His attention to detail put him in charge of our paperwork dealing with government authorities, banks and so on.

My eldest brother was the social one. He liked going out, so if it was household shopping, it was he who would willingly take it up. If it were delivering a file or papers to someone, it was he who would do it. He was a charmer, making friends and attracting girls with absolute ease. He was fashion conscious, had the looks of a model and never liked a crease to show on any shirt he wore.

Both of them loved acting. Dilip was once a part of the Theatre Action Group referred to as TAG. Duji was a part of his college theatre society and went on to be a member of Chingari, a group led by K. Madavane. He was more serious about theatre, seeing it as storytelling and an alternative means to say something. He experimented a lot and even acted as a woman.

I was the homebody, feeling safe in familiar surroundings. I was happier helping in the kitchen or even sweeping the floors if we had no help. There was a different kind of thrill that I experienced in preparing a meal or dusting or finding filth under the bed and sweeping it out using a broom.

Yet, even if all these 'activities' called for a lot of movement and exercise, I was the one who was constantly growing in size and becoming more and more socially uncomfortable. The few times that I would walk down to the local market, I could sense people staring at me. Some even passed comments suggesting that I was responsible for a food crisis, if there was one. I ate all three meals and in between also filled myself up with chocolates, namkeen and even Maggi noodles.

I was close to a hundred-kg then. If I had to check my weight, someone else had to read the scale as my belly obstructed my view. Clothes were another problem. There weren't any Indian brands that made my size. I had a couple of ready-made shirts that were rejects from an uncle's garment export house whose main market was the US—a country where my size was not unusual. All my trousers and jeans were tailored at Mohan Singh Place in the CP area, a market where my brothers went if they wanted something copied.

By that time, I had developed a disregard for any sport other than what was part of our school curriculum. Dilip and Duji, in contrast, played cricket, football and were always out there in the colony. Dilip was the fittest of us three. Duji was neither thin nor fat, he was somewhere in the middle but was active.

Towards the end of class nine, in early 1986, after a long discussion between Ma and my brothers, I was literally pulled out from my room and dragged outside to play the most popular sport—cricket—with my brothers and their friends. The reason was simple and precise: I was growing too fat and I could not live a life moving from one room to another (including the kitchen and all the other domestic spaces) without having a life outside the four walls of our house.

Since I was the youngest in Dilip and Duji's group of friends who played cricket, it was always me who ran after the ball, searched for it in drains or entered homes where the ball might have landed after it was hit out of the park. I rarely got to bat or bowl or take any decision whatsoever. Fortunately, no one pulled my pants down.

The first few days out on the field left me with a body ache like never before. Every muscle hurt, reminding me of how rusty I had become. None of this mattered to my brothers or Ma, all of whom were thrilled that I was finally stepping out of the house after school and on holidays. In time, even I started enjoying these outings. The muscles stopped aching and once in a while I got to bat and bowl as well.

I started to follow cricket more closely. Sunil Gavaskar became my batting hero and I liked Ravi Shastri for his bowling, height and style. I think I related to Shastri a lot more as he was a left-handed bowler and a right-handed batsman. I was the same and even tried to copy his high-arm action around the wicket and his style of defence as a batsman.

Soon, for me, cricket became a lot bigger than I had ever imagined. It went beyond physical exercise as it integrated me into the general scheme of things that boys did, particularly middle-class boys. I was now a part of a regular clan of people, carrying some titbit of the sport back home to the dining table or kitchen where we all spent a lot of our time as a single family unit. Even picking up a wicket was a huge achievement for me and something to boast about and narrate.

Like three of us boys, Ma too started sharing what her day had been like. With the course in naturopathy behind her, she started a free service operating out of our garage that we had turned into a clinic. It was the realization of her childhood dream as she had always wanted to be like Florence Nightingale and heal people. I, though, wasn't one of her patients as it required too much discipline. She would offer help and, once in a while, provoke me into a realization of how unhealthy I was, but she never imposed her 'prescription' on me, choosing to wait 'until I was ready'.

As Ma pursued her passion, my brothers talked about what

they wished to do. Dilip who was doing his bachelor's in commerce wanted to follow the marketing route which meant an MBA was his next step. Duji was doing his BA in economics, intending to build on that with an MA and a PhD. I had no such clarity, not yet but eventually was expected to walk down a career path.

We were very comfortable in our lives thinking ahead, oblivious to the changes happening around us. Living off the rent we received from our ground floor since the day we moved to Delhi, we never foresaw a situation where finding a tenant would ever be difficult. Most tenants, foreign companies included, had started practising 'illegal' arrangements, that is, part payment in cash and the balance in cheque.

As a family, we had decided that cash payments were a big no-no. I remember Ma repeatedly saying this to broker after broker and to potential tenant after tenant. We could not go against the principles my father had set. He had written a lot against black money and the cash economy (none of which I understood at that age)

In short, we were facing a crisis of no income with a two-storey house to maintain, bills to pay and fees to be deposited. Looking back, I realize how this situation brought our family closer and our ability to earn money even though we had no experience of working.

Dilip, who had recently qualified himself in various operating skills in computers, began teaching, bringing in some money. Duji started tutoring juniors. Ma, against her wishes, levied a consulting fee to some of her very wealthy patients. And I sold cakes and puddings directly to friends or at festivals and fairs held in and around our colony. I also put together cassettes of dance music and offered them at a price, selling them under the name SDR Recordings.

We cut back on the use of our Fiat Premier Padmini car that we had acquired about a year ago. We mostly walked or took a DTC bus with the autorickshaw being a luxury. We sold our rarely used large air cooler (which, in any case, we couldn't use due to Duji's asthma) and went about selling anything that seemed pointless to have.

Some eleven months later, our austerity measures were over as we found a tenant who was ready for a clean deal The Fiat was in greater use. Duji stopped tutoring with the exception of a student or two who insisted on learning from him. Dilip turned his teaching income into pocket money. And I stopped mixing music and selling cakes and puddings, unless there was a special request, while Ma reduced the number of paying patients.

What didn't change was our huddling every night in Ma's room to use that single air conditioner. It was a pattern that I carried forward for over a decade, after both my brothers had embarked on their own pursuits of education and marriage, and left me alone with the privacy of 'their' room.

Chapter Seven

THERE WAS A sense of ease as I entered class ten because the set of students were the same as in the previous year and I was familiar with the school, its system and the teachers. To have the same set of classmates in consecutive years was a first since Mumbai, making it easier for me to build some friendships.

What was different in me as a person was that I was no longer a bully pushing my weight around creating fear among others, nor was I leading a group to battle another one. My tummy held up too, barring the first few months in the city and the instances of health problems became rare with time. And most importantly, I was now having conversations, sitting together in the same row for over a year with a group of three other boys. We shared our tiffins and participated in the occasional naughtiness that landed us in trouble with our teachers.

The tallest one, Mangesh, was the most studious amongst us and preferred to be cautious when it came to violating the rules in class. Harsh was studious too but naughty. Sunjoy was neither overtly studious nor naughty and he was the one who always had unusual food that we all craved for. A few of his relatives were part owners of a Bengali sweet shop in South Delhi that was known for sandesh and samosas made in ghee.

We were chatty, and thus got reprimanded ever so often by one teacher or the other. Occasionally, after school, we walked down to Central Market in Lajpat Nagar or to South Extension for general mischief and merrymaking.

Even though I enjoyed the camaraderie I shared with my friends and liked going to school, I did not find a single guy or girl attractive enough, which was quite unlike Mumbai or Kolkata. What was also different, and I don't know whether it was a cultural thing or had something to do with my batch specifically, none of us ever visited each other's homes, not unless it was a birthday, or some 'occasion' as they called it.

Also, I am not sure if I missed them coming over as such because there were other dimensions emerging in my life.

Dilip introduced me to Shabnam—a friend of his—who insisted I meet her brother, Nitin. He was five years younger than me, slim and slightly pale. He was born and brought up in Delhi and had many friends in the colony. He wasn't an authoritative person, yet he had a way of persisting and could manage to convince the young of the colony to come out and play cricket or badminton or even tennis with him.

While he spoke fluent English, Hindi was the chosen language at his home. His mother was a doting one, warm and friendly. She and I enjoyed talking about food, particularly recipes for cakes. She always told me that I would be a helpful husband to the lady I would eventually marry. Nitin's father was a happy-go-lucky person. He was closely associated with Korean radio and was always ready for some media and political gossip. In the years to come, he and I had many discussions on news and business, criticizing cronies of governments and media.

Nitin's eldest sister, Neelam, was aspiring to become a doctor and went on to practise in the US. Shabnam was pursuing multiple courses related to soft skills and finally took on teaching as a profession. She and I became great friends and it was normal for both of us to manage the kitchen on several of Nitin's birthday parties.

Meeting Nitin contributed significantly in changing my

impression of the city, something that my friends from school had started to do too. He was friendly, outgoing, easy to get along with, enjoyed sharing books and comics and came over without waiting for an 'occasion', which was an instinct of informality I had seen in a few friends of Dilip and Duji. He had a sweet tooth which meant both of us could share chocolates almost every day after our session of sports. What he loved though was sleeping and slept till late on weekends or during the holidays.

I, on the other hand, had become an early riser which was a huge change from the lazy boy I had been in childhood. On weekends, I was happy to leave home early, at 5.30 a.m., to wake him up in the hope that by around 6.15 a.m. we could gather a few other people to play cricket or badminton, which was a game that I had been introduced to by Nitin who was probably one of the best players in his school and in Gulmohar Park. I started learning the game, not allowing my large frame to become an impediment, and eventually became a pretty good doubles partner to Nitin. In fact, my size helped me cover the net in a reasonably effective manner!

Our love for the game was such that we rehabilitated a cracked cement court very close to his home. We got fresh new poles and nets and searched for a way to get an electrical connection so that we could play in the evenings too.

It was Nitin's persuasion powers that helped us get a connection. He pitched our story in Hindi to a resident who lived almost adjacent to the court and explained that a dhobi in the by-lane between the court and their home had a line to their house. The dhobi was put in charge of passing us the line and often helped in keeping the court as clean as possible at a nominal charge. We, of course, had now become friendly with the generous resident and the dhobi.

Every morning, his charpai would lie close to our court with himself or someone else from his family, sleeping on it. We rarely paid attention to such details until one day as we were waiting for two more friends to arrive to play doubles, Nitin pointed towards the man lying on the charpai. 'Just look,' he said in a loud whisper.

There lay someone we hadn't seen before, a brown-skinned man—with sunken cheeks, short black hair and square set jaw—who was so thin that his ribs and shoulder blades were clearly visible. He was wearing a sleeveless white vest that had browned with use and sweat. It had holes reflecting wear and tear and most likely the wearer's un-affordability to look after it. His boxer-like underwear had faded blue stripes and was loose, as expected. There was also a boner that stood up... and stood out.

'He must be dreaming,' said one of our friends as he entered the court and saw what we were staring at, transfixed. They broke into giggles, trying to control their laughter, and this sight soon turned into a gossip item amongst our larger group. I smiled and looked fixedly at what seemed to be a long large penis under that underwear. I said very little except that 'he must be sexually active, dreaming of someone or maybe this is all he gets—the morning wood!'

I reached that spot every morning for several days, earlier than normal and before I'd go and wake up Nitin, with the hope that I would see the same sight again. I was lucky just about once out of almost a week, as the man on that bed was never seen again.

What this incident did for our whole group was to allow us to talk about sex—not sex as an act but who liked whom and whether we had girlfriends. Rahul, a very handsome and witty friend of Nitin living a few lanes away, popular for his good looks and charm, spoke freely about his likes and his following of girls. He often said that Nitin was not strong or masculine enough to attract a woman on his own and thus it would be his parents who would find him a girl.

Feeling compelled to say something, I claimed that girls had come up to me many times, but I believed that there was one true love for everyone and I wanted to wait for the right person and marriage, until then I was happy 'jerking off'.

This claim was partly true. I had resumed masturbating, sometimes trying to recall the face of the Chinese boy in Kolkata. If not him, it was Jermaine Jackson and most recently, it was the towering penis of the 'dhobi man' that had captured my imagination, conjuring up enough delight to allow me the little pleasures that I treasured privately in my toilet.

There was another strange habit that I seemed to be getting into soon after seeing the 'dhobi man'. I had started eyeing men, hoping to spot a bulge or an evidence of a penis. I did this at school and even in markets. Across the street from my home, was a bus stop. While waiting for a bus or the autos that drove by, I would be busy scanning men, looking at their faces, below their waists and between their legs and sometimes at a rounded backside. I was also enamoured by the dangling penis shaking under the loose briefs that labourers wore.

I did not give these incidents much thought initially but soon I did. I remember lying in bed wondering why I had developed such a dirty and awful habit. These questions led me to curtail the number of times I was masturbating. In fact, I even tried to erase the memories of Jermaine Jackson, the Chang-like boy from Kolkata and the 'dhobi man'.

I had heard many conversations that my brothers had with their friends about their attractions, dates or parties, but they never referred to men, their crotches, faces or organs. I would hear them talk excitedly about some female movie star or some girl in their college, or someone in our colony, but it was always a woman who aroused their interest. Even Rahul spoke of women and his hard-ons and how he dreamt of them. Nitin, although muted in his expression, would also talk of some girl he was attracted to in school.

Even though I felt that such conversations were, in any case, dirty to have, I was convinced my acts—even though private—were sinful. I constantly wondered, 'Why men? Why so much masturbation?'

Troubled by these thoughts churning in my mind, I turned to *The Naked Ape* once again, while I was alone at home. I went slowly, page by page, searching for the words 'male', 'sexuality', 'attraction', 'pervert' and I don't know what else. I kept the book with me for several days, snatching whatever time I got alone to read it.

Finally, I seemed to have hit the nail on the head. I found some paragraphs referring to homosexuality and from what I understood from reading the text, it occurred, at times, in the absence of the opposite sex. I penned down what I found from the book—homosexual behaviour is also seen in situations where the ideal sexual object (a member of the opposite sex) is unavailable.

The fact that I had no girlfriend and had never been motivated enough to seek or find anyone, the opposite sex was resultantly absent from my life. The only girls I had met were my cousins, classmates or the friends of my brothers. The book, from what I understood, suggested that what I was going through was just a phase and once the absence of the opposite sex would end, that is, when some girl would come into my life or I would get married, the attraction for men—their faces, crotches and butts—would go away on its own.

I concluded with relief that consequently I would stop masturbating and follow the normal path of marriage and children, just like my parents, aunts and uncles. And therefore, homosexuality was bound to fade away!

Chapter Eight

THE NEXT COUPLE of years, after I passed my class ten board examinations, were rather sedate, calm and pleasant. While my grades in class ten were nothing to write home about, I did not fail, which in itself was a relief. The grades, however, left me with a 'Hobson's choice', that is arts—a stream that did not have the same prestige attached to it as commerce or science.

There was a newness to my class; after all, there were now only a handful of familiar students and many new ones. I had a feeling that the 'gang' I was a part of would soon 'disband'. Mangesh, Harsh, Sunjoy and I would meet on and off at recess or even after school but our distinct streams of arts, commerce and science seemed to push us away from the proximity we had shared once.

Strangely and positively, none of these fresh dynamics troubled me. They were making new friends and so was I.

I had one new and special friend, Moushumi, who went on to become the only FAPS schoolmate I remained in touch with. She was a singer and an elocutionist and became the head girl during our last year in school. She did not mind missing classes or even pulling me out of a study period for some unimportant matter using the privilege of being the head girl. She had a spirit that transcended the idea of what a 'good' or 'disciplined' student was supposed to be and that in itself was charming.

Her passion for music—our common area of interest—was a key connection between the two of us. She was aware of Pink Floyd to Bob Dylan, making me feel pretty much at home with her. She and I put across several arguments before our then principal to bring music into our school system. We won and by the time we were in class twelve, FAPS was competing in inter-school competitions besides having our own little shows in school.

Her popularity gave her access to some of the most beautiful boys I had ever seen and I wondered how I had never noticed them all these years I had been in FAPS. There was Roger who played the guitar and Arnie who sang. She liked both of them and I remember her saying 'Isn't Roger cute?' but I thought they were both good-looking.

Arnie was short, had a skeletal frame, dark complexion, a wide smile and large eyes that seemed happy all the time. I think he was in class nine at that time and was a huge fan of Michael Jackson, trying to moonwalk as a show of his dedication to the huge star. Roger was around my height, had a wheatish complexion, gentle smile, nice round cheeks, thick hair and kind eyes, making him very attractive.

Moushumi's sense of freedom meant she did not need to rush home by a certain time, could go watch films when she wanted and ate food just about anywhere. When I refused staying out beyond 4 or 5 p.m., she would taunt me chanting, 'Mama's boy!' I never liked that remark. I would counter her but she never stopped calling me 'mama's boy'.

I don't know why I always got irked when she said this. I guess such comments questioned my ability to be decisive and a strong man which, in turn, showed that I was not in control of my own life. With hindsight, maybe it was the general conditioning, a result of patriarchy, where men yielded power and ruled their own lives and being anything but that masculine person was considered a weakness. After all, if a woman such as Moushumi could be free to make simple choices like staying out beyond a certain hour, how could a man like me not be able to do the same?

Still, she and I remained good friends. What she always quipped about was how I remembered the clothes and accessories any of our female teachers had ever worn. What can I say? This was how it was. Every time someone asked whether X or Y teacher had come to school, and if I had spotted that person, I would say yes and then proceed to tell them the colour of her sari, whether her hair was open or in braids, and even the colour of her heels.

I did this inadvertently in a most natural manner and gave such details to provide evidence to back my answer. It was only years later that I realized that these were considered unique features, an attribute often seen in some gay men. However, at that time Moushumi thought that maybe fashion or photography was a line I should consider because of my 'attention to detail'. I, of course, had no view on that.

But she had a very clear idea about where she was and what her future should be like. She would go down the social sector route (social service as we called it then), working for people and probably even teaching. Some of our other classmates—men, that is—were moving into their family business. Girls, most of them, seemed resigned to marriage and had no clarity of what they wished to do, although a few are now running their own business.

Even I was vague and was unable to project beyond a BA. 'And after that?' Moushumi asked. I shrugged my shoulders not knowing what I might do. She found my response strange and suggested that I should be more like my brothers—sorted. Actually, that was exactly how she was too. And that is why her understanding of my brothers was quite accurate.

Duji completed his BA in economics from Delhi University and was soon in JNU doing his MA in economics and had more or less identified a foreign university for his PhD—a plan that had not changed at all over the years. Dilip, who had completed his BCom and a specialization in marketing from Xavier's in Mumbai, was already working with one of the largest English dailies in their

Response Department.

He had also met his love, Sonu, while working in that organization. Soon, they turned their office romance into marriage. This decision was taken just weeks before I was to complete my class twelve, at a time when anxieties of exams prevailed. And the marriage was to be days after my last paper. Unlike the much-talked-about Punjabi weddings of Delhi, this was a low-key affair. It was a Sikh wedding held in the morning with maybe around 100–125 people in attendance followed by a reception that had more or less the same number, held at the India International Centre.

Dilip and Sonu spent only a few days at home with us in Gulmohar Park. Soon, they moved to South Extension, getting their personal space and started building a life of their own. Duji, even though he wasn't technically a hostler at JNU, managed to spend most of his time on campus staying in someone or the other's room. He seemed to enjoy testing the limits of university norms not just when it came to hostel rules but also in the case of the rights of students. As it was, he was already an active member of one of the parties at JNU, and entered a certain kind of politics that satiated his ideologies.

I, as is the pattern of our education system, had got into my first year of college after struggling to get admission given my class twelve marks which averaged at under 70 per cent. It was Duji who ran around North and South Campuses, finally helping me secure a place in Bhagat Singh College which was then based in Govindpuri, a college that stood out for its commerce faculty rather than anything else, certainly not English for sure—the course I got admitted to.

We had a class of some twenty students, not many of whom seemed to instinctively speak English. This made me a favourite of sorts with some of our teachers and also a bit popular amongst the small batch that we were. I was also reasonably regular with my attendance to college, unlike many others. In fact, there were several occasions when the teachers cancelled our class since there were just one or two of us in attendance. As a result, I would sit around the very small building of the college, reading through books, having cups of tea or just staring aimlessly at nothing.

The college had a varied mix of students coming from different parts of Delhi, representing a blend of language influences, cultures and economic backgrounds. The more affluent ones and those who did well in their school board examinations were in the college's prestigious commerce stream. The rest were in other courses including English. Till now in all the schools that I had attended, there was a largely specific band of students that were joined together by income, proximity to the school and some commonality of backgrounds and culture.

This change was fascinating, often leaving me staring at the diversity before my eyes. I had never seen such a mix of men in one place in all my life. Sometimes my eyes were fixed on a group or just on one person, often not realizing that I was staring and probably my stare could be noticed or felt or considered rude.

I recall one incident related to a senior. He was a wheatish-to-fair-complexioned muscular man in a tight T-shirt and denims with gelled hair, kohl-lined eyes and a stud in his left ear. He seemed to be an important person or someone with clout as all it took was for him to snap his fingers and the canteen man would deliver tea or whatever else he wanted to have. He also appeared to lead the pack as everyone in that group always seemed to be listening to him. I was focused entirely on him for over a minute or two I think, maybe even longer.

There was something beautiful about him but I did not know how absorbed I was by him, noticing nothing, not even the fact that he was now standing almost before me. I was three steps up, in a corridor while he was at the ground level, with an outstretched hand that was between my legs, touching my testicles, almost holding them.

'*Kya chahiye* (What do you want)?' he asked.

His eyes looked stern and his voice was curt. Taken aback by his gesture and frightened by his question and the fact that he was aware of my focus on him, I hurriedly replied 'nothing', pretending I had not noticed him until he spoke to me. I quickly started retracing my steps and turning away. It was then that I noticed a shift in him. His sternness had gone and was replaced with a smile that seemed to say he knew something, maybe the answer to his question.

I saw him on and off in college; our eyes would meet, he would smile but that was all. We never spoke to each other. I felt awkward since the day his hand felt my groin. I did not know what to think of it but I did dream of him, and even masturbated at times remembering his touch. And even now I can recall his face with full clarity and feel his hand where it had been.

But that day I had made a vow to myself that I would never stare at a person the way I had ever again!

Chapter Nine

AS THAT YEAR progressed, so did my waist and weight, crossing the forty-four-inch and a hundred-kg mark, respectively. No activity in terms of sport seemed to help reduce the inches and kilos. Both my body and I had become very stubborn. Ma was worried and tried to ration my meals. My brothers were not at all amused and reprimanded me every few days.

Ma went one step further and proclaimed that no new clothes would be tailored for me and even the cost of alterations would be borne by me, from my pocket money. This literally shrunk the options I had in my little cupboard. Of the many shirts I owned, only five or six tailor-made ones fitted me and just one ready-made went around my waist, a blue- and white-striped, half-sleeve shirt.

This shirt was my favourite mainly because it had not been tailored and put me at par with most of my friends and brothers who had a wardrobe of branded clothes. My bond with this shirt was so great that the day it tore—it ripped from the sides as I struggled to button the shirt—I cried and decided that I had to lose weight. The shirt had already been through intense wear and tear due to my shapeless flabby frame grazing against the weakening cotton every time I wore it.

I ran to Ma and pleaded for her help in setting me on the right course. Knowing my past indiscipline, she said that I would be taken to a hospital for tests if I did not follow her regime. I was scared of hospitals. I did not like the smell of them or the sight of a needle or blood. I asked for fifteen days to show results and my commitment to weight loss.

Ma put me on a diet that allowed me all meals but with restrictions on what I ate. From a person who enjoyed meat at almost every meal, I was now consuming a lot more vegetables, juices and fruits. I even added certain exercises to my daily routine. In around two months, I was ten kg down. By the fourth month, I had lost another five kg, changing my wardrobe with new off-the-shelf clothes as well as altering a large number of my old shirts and pants.

After many years, I could see my double chin reducing. My shoulder blades were becoming visible—something I had always found attractive in other men. I could also feel my ribs. The compliments on the visible change in my appearance gave me a lot more confidence. I looked younger, my skin was smoother and fairer and I felt more alert, as if I was a changed person.

At the end of that year in college, Ma and Duji decided I should move to Sri Venkateswara College as it had a superior faculty for English. The process was not very complicated and the transfer came through within weeks. However, my growing confidence that was being powered by my shrinking waist did not help me in finding my footing in the new college.

My pass percentage of around fifty was poor compared to most of the students in my new class. Besides, there were already several groups within the class, all built over the past year or from the schools they came from. I was an outsider from an inferior college 'that didn't even have its own campus'—a remark that was mockingly made many a times. In short, I had been a big fish in a small pond while at Bhagat Singh College and now I was a small one in a big pond and was completely lost.

I had more conversations with teachers than students. Some of them were known to Uma masi who told me to give her reference. This was a saving grace of sorts as I at least had someone to talk to.

However, breaks between classes or the general lunch recess were often a lonely affair. I could not get myself to crack any of the groups. My regularity of attendance dropped and I would just wander around South Campus, head to a library and read, stroll around quiet parks or just go back home.

This pattern did not change, not even with the progress of time. I literally slipped into the second year with an under 50 per cent average and struggled throughout the third year. I did, however, make greater efforts at studying by using guidebooks and taking help from a tutor closer to the annual examinations.

Ma was unaware of my falling attendance but, she knew about my marks and was very upset with my results. She felt the increased hours I spent at home studying, making notes and then the tuitions would help in improving my grades, which they did. In the months to come, I returned to the 50 per cent level in my internal exams in the third year.

As was the case in most homes, or at least in the ones I knew, the third year in college was by when one should have had a clear idea of career prospects with the preparation beginning the year before. Dilip and Sonu led such conversations with me as they were more aware of the world than Ma. Duji, on the other hand, was too engrossed in his studies and preparing to move to a foreign university for a PhD, to give inputs. And I, as usual, was brilliantly oblivious.

I felt I should become like Ma—a naturopath, working from home. In fact, her clinic hours were increasing as more and more patients sought her time and expertise. She had even expanded into the areas of dance therapy, aromatherapy and reflexology, solving a variety of ailments of her growing list of patients. This option was ruled out by Ma herself who said it was an uncertain profession and for her it was still a hobby.

Dilip felt that maybe journalism or something related with writing was a line I should consider as I had written features on music for publications such as the *Sunday Observer*. 'This could be your calling,' he had remarked. We never discussed this any further although he did extract a promise from me that I would study hard and keep my mind open to options beyond Ma's line of work.

I was, however, enamoured by Ma's profession. She was committed, opening the clinic around 10.30 in the morning soon after returning from her two-hour studies of old Indian scriptures. She took a short break for lunch and reopened her clinic around 4 p.m. till 7.30 in the evening. While I admired her discipline, my greatest temptation for a job like hers was the fact that I would be able to be at home, serve and, in a way, be in charge of all I did.

If there was a fear about the work she did it was the routine and diligence. It was long hours of work, if one also added the early morning rush to reach her study group. It was during this time that she finally decided to look for full-time domestic help beyond the cook and cleaning-woman we already had. Employing a young girl or boy was out of the question, even though they were the most easily available option that seemed to knock on our door. Ma believed that any youngster should study, build some skills and work in an organized space beyond a home.

After months of searching, she finally buckled under pressure from a family friend and selected a boy who was soon going to turn eighteen. The only condition put by Ma was that he had to study and would be admitted in a school soon after the summer vacations. It was the month of May then.

The boy's name was Sufal. He hailed from a village in Bihar. It was an unexpected relief to have him around, particularly during the summer vacations. He and I would talk about food, his village, cinema and music. I cannot remember how our conversations led to love songs from Bollywood or how we started acting them out. We described the setting of hills and trees, the running around them, the haystacks that couples fell on and even the kissing that was never shown.

Sufal surprised me when he said a lot of this was common in his village, particularly how haystacks were often used for lovemaking. He asked if I had a girlfriend and I said no. '*Kaise aadmi ho* (What kind of man are you)?' he said, wondering what kind of person I was given that I was over twenty years old. '*Kya aapne kisi ko kiss kiya hai* (Have you ever kissed someone)?' I asked. He nodded his head proudly and said, '*Picturon mein jaise* (Just like in the films).'

I was standing in front of my bed, the back of my knee touching the wooden bed frame. He was in front of me and was sharing the nuggets of his sex life quite liberally. I thought I was living in the modern, liberal Capital city but look at him and his experiences; a boy from rural India.

Sufal, in his uninhibited style, nudged me a bit with his chest over mine and I fell onto the bed, my face very close to his. In less than a second, I think, his lips were touching mine. I instinctively—I did not even know that I had this instinct though—let his tongue into my mouth and moments later, pushed mine into his. Our eyes closed, we were kissing like in the English movies I had seen. '*Aisa hota hain* (That is how we do it),' he said with a smile after a while, picking himself up as well as the duster cloth that had fallen on the floor.

I smiled. I was delighted at this surprising new turn that my life had taken, not knowing then that how this encounter had sowed the seed for what was going to be an unexpected bonding.

Every other day, after Ma went off for her study classes and before the part-time servants arrived, Sufal and I would chat, laugh and be intimate. We had become 'partners in crime' managing the little time we had together, with me taking on the dusting so that our escapades didn't come in the way of completing the few tasks he had on hand.

I am not sure how to define the bond we shared but it was friendship for sure. There were times when we used to start talking about films and end while discussing how Biharis were seen as poor and backward outside his state. He talked about his village set-up, the family he belonged to, the daily grind and irrelevance of education as farming was the main occupation in his village. '*Maine kabhi yeh nahi socha tha ki mujhe koi dost milega is shahar mein* (I never thought I would find a friend like you in this city),' he whispered. I looked at him, his eyes had a softness that I hadn't seen before.

As the weeks went by and the peak of summer enveloped Delhi, Sufal was expected to prepare for school. This meant sitting with me after dinner, studying under my guidance. Ma would sleep off while Sufal and I would chat. He told me how being a man gave him a huge advantage which was to sleep and have sex with both men and women—a privilege he believed he would hold even after he got married. I never thought such a life even existed.

Our conversations, playful banter, open smiles and hands that were free to arouse each other, basically the regularity of coexistence within the four walls of home—all of this, I think, gave me a sense of what a relationship could be like without the defined roles that couples typically had. What it also did was keep me from staying out till late, that is, if I ever ventured out with friends. That late night hug with Sufal to say goodnight and the occasional kiss had become a passionate ritual that I prayed would remain.

He was undoubtedly adventurous and a man with guts, someone who was confident and sure of himself, at least within our space. He would often come from behind, hold me and not let go, urging all the while to stop reading and spend time with him. Sometimes that would lead to lustful encounter and sometimes, just a silent cup of tea. He was fearless enough to bend down to my crotch as I drove the car when we went out shopping one afternoon. '*Kaun dekh sakta hain* (Who can see this)?' he said looking up, as I half-heartedly asked him to refrain. Dangerous as such an act was, the pleasure of unexpected encounters often allowed me to take such chances, forgetting the risks.

For him it may have been what we now call a work-life balance or business with pleasure, but for me it was life. I was the student and Sufal was the guide, the magician who had a way of adding life to my life.

All of a sudden, one hot day that May, Sufal was called back home. He had no advance information about why he needed to return to his village. I was heartbroken. I was so used to his presence, his body, his naughty eyes and at times, that wicked smile. I was attached to what we had, whatever it was.

On the eve of his departure, we both had moist eyes, choking as we spoke, expressing how used to we had become to each other. He said he would be back in some time, not indicating when. We hugged each other for several minutes, saying nothing, ending it all with a kiss. As he left for his room he said, '*Aap bahut achhe ho, main aap ko yaad karunga* (You are very nice, I will remember you).' I held back my emotions, the tears that were waiting to flow.

The next afternoon, the day he was supposed to leave, he looked visibly sad. The chirpiness, the big smile on his face and the joy in his eyes were all gone. I think at that moment I believed we were in love, and that thought somehow satisfied me, convincing me that this wasn't and couldn't be the end.

He left and I reluctantly headed out to the local club for a tennis match I had that evening. Distracted and unhappy, I tried to conceal the occasional moistness of my eyes by pretending to clean my sweat on the T-shirt sleeve. I could not concentrate and lost a match that I would have normally won. That night, I could hardly sleep. I sat up, pulled out an inland letter—a commonly used form of post—and wrote to Sufal. I told him I was already missing him and was looking forward to his return. I described a possible future for him in Delhi. I asked him to send me his local phone number and to reply soon.

Over two weeks went by without any information from him. I

wrote again. This attempt was futile too as another few weeks went by without any information from him. I remember Ma saying she doubted that he would return at all or any time soon.

I secretly hoped that her reading was not true.

Sufal neither answered my letters ever, nor returned. My sorrow remained confined to my heart as I was unable to share it with anyone. Who would have understood in any case?

Chapter Ten

AFTER COMPLETING MY college with an ordinary percentage of a little over fifty, I was out hunting for a job. I had no interest in further studies and there was no pressure to do a postgraduation as long as I found a job soon enough. Thank God for that! Dilip and Duji kept their eyes open for job interviews feeling that I would be best off doing something related to the English language such as journalism or publishing.

As luck would have it, Penguin Books India had an advertisement for the post of an editorial assistant. This was an entry-level role supporting the editorial department that selected manuscripts, engaged with authors, edited books and proofread copy, leading to the final production. I went through a written test followed by an interview with the editor which somehow went off very well. I, who conversed little except at home and with friends in my colony, was literally speaking throughout the interview. Duji had told me to ask questions so that I could know my role and the job profile. He said that this would not just bring clarity of what was expected of me but it would also suggest that I was interested.

I was soon part of the publishing house, sitting with a small team, comprising mostly women, in a South Delhi colony. The room was generally filled with cigarette smoke, which left my eyes red. It took me weeks to adjust to such an environment. The first few days were spent on learning the basics of editing including the house style and the usage of the signs to mark out edits. What followed was a mix of proofing, engaging with DTP printers and even taking phone calls in the absence of a receptionist.

While I was in no position to gauge my performance, I did feel important when asked to help even if it were to pick up a paper from the photocopying machine. At home, however, returning with a pile of papers and files symbolized how busy I was, and therefore an important cog in the office machinery.

What was enduring, in its own way, was the friendly environment led, if not created, by the chatty and somewhat flamboyant Sudha Sadanand. While I did not report to her directly, her seniority in the organization and experience as an editor made her a reference point of sorts. She was the only one who asked me about my hobbies and whether I was enjoying my job. I told her about my interests in music and cooking and that I was happy at work. I, however, was not clear whether I was happy doing what I was in my role.

One conversation led to another and I was soon making cookies, baking cakes and bringing them to office. I soon got popular for my culinary skills rather than for my role as an editorial assistant. One day, Sudha came up to my desk and kissed me on my cheek, leaving behind a bright red impression of her lips. I was taken aback and embarrassed, not knowing how to respond. This was the first time a woman had kissed me. 'You've never been kissed,' Sudha said with a smile, using her pallu to wipe off the lipstick from my cheek before walking back to her terminal.

I did not know what to make of that kiss but finally asked her why had she done that. 'For one it was the lovely pudding and the other was your sweet behaviour, a convent boy, who I felt needed a bit of opening up,' she said. What was I to open up to, I wondered and put that incident behind me.

As I got more books to provide support on, I was sometimes heading to a DTP printer in the evening or to an author's home to deliver proofs of his or her manuscript. Even though I felt responsible, I grew more and more disinterested in work. But I realized that I had to hold on to my role and work for at least a year in the same company; it was something that most people did before switching jobs.

And good I did so!

One evening, as I entered the driveway of my home, a young boy rushed out from the ground floor house that we had recently given on rent to a multinational bank that was running a chummery or a hostel from there. He reminded me of the Chinese boy in Kolkata. He was fair and slim, and did not have any hair on his arms or other visible parts of the body. He didn't have a moustache or stubble and his face was lit up with a cute yet naughty smile.

The papers under my arms had fallen as I was startled by the suddenness of his appearance. He stopped, looked at me and helped me in picking up the papers. He smiled and so did I. He headed to the servants' quarters that was being used by our tenants and I went up the stairs to our floor.

The next morning, as I was leaving for work, I looked for him, hoping he would appear on the driveway or in the shared passage that led to the ground floor premises and the staircase going up to our home. He was nowhere to be seen.

What I did not know then was that he was soon going to be employed with us. Suresh, the man in charge of the chummery had asked Ma to give him—his cousin—some work. Murli was his name, belonging to the Pokhara region of Nepal. He had just reached Delhi a few days ago. For Suresh, Ma's condition that he study and pick up some skills was a huge relief.

Full of energy, a big fan of Bollywood music and keen to be a karate kid, Murli had a pleasant and chirpy presence. I looked forward to interacting with him every day on my return from office. '*Kaise ho* (How are you)?' he would shout out from the top of the stairs as I walked up after a day's work. If I was tired and told him not to bother me, he would turn up the volume of the music playing in the kitchen on a two-in-one we had, '*Aapne ye dance dekha hai* (Have you seen this dance)?' Then he would try to mimic Akshaye Khanna or Saif Ali Khan which would leave me in splits.

If I was preoccupied, he would serve me a cup of tea even if I had not asked for one, '*Wah Taj boliye na*!' He would smile and say, '*Oye Zakir bhai, muskarao to sahi! Aap sheher wale tension bahut lete hain, Pokhara aaiye na mere saath* (Hey Zakir bhai, at least smile. You city dwellers take a lot of tension, come to Pokhara with me).' He had repeatedly asked me to come with him to his village. '*Bas hum dono, ekdum masti* (Just the two of us having fun),' he would say in his affectionate manner that always took me offguard, drawing me towards him.

He and I would often speak about Bollywood and music. He would tell me about Pokhara and I would share a little about my family and our past. From music, we moved to wrestling and even started mock-fighting with each other, with no specified rules. I would pin him down and hold him there. '*Karate seekhne do na, main aap ka protection karoonga* (Let me learn karate, I will protect you),' he would repeatedly express this desire which I could never fulfil. On occasions our hands touched each other's in a very intimate manner, or our legs would be entwined with each other's, and at those moments he would only say, '*Kya ho raha hai, bhai* (What is happening, brother)?' His smiles would turn to stares and I would watch him closely not knowing what to expect. These evening 'battles' became habitual and were a lot of fun. After a few wins, I preferred to lie down and let him take charge, giving him a sense of victory.

One day, when both of us were lying on the floor, exhausted, he commented, '*Aap bahut strong ho, kya aadmi ho yaar* (You are a very strong man).' He further went on to use the word *mardangi* or masculinity suggesting I could easily find anyone I wanted. '*Mardangi ka matlab ye hi nahin hota* (Masculinity doesn't only mean this),' I remember telling him. I also remember how this led to discussing the male organ, its size and strength: the penis as an important attribute of a man and the fact that a strong man did not mind displaying it. *'Mera bahut chota hai, main nahin dikha sakta hoon, main shy hoon* (Mine is very small, I cannot show it, I am shy),' he had said looking down as I gave him a few seconds to see mine. He looked curiously, raised his eyebrows, and then smiled with mischievousness reflecting in his eyes. I was hoping he would touch it but he did not. *'Wah yaar* (Wow, friend),' is all he said.

Our friendship did not have any definition but we enjoyed every moment that we spent together, that is between the time I returned from work and dinner when Ma returned from her clinic.

Even the job I wished to quit had provided me with an alibi. On some evenings, I would leave home claiming I had some work and then pick up Murli after he had wound up for the night, which was around 9–9.30 p.m. We would go on drives around Delhi and sometimes have ice creams or sundaes from Nirula's Defence Colony outlet under the flyover. He enjoyed these outings as we listened to music and he could talk endlessly about his childhood and his interest in sports such as football and of course martial arts. Apparently, he had seen *Karate Kid* back home in Nepal and had become a fan.

From a mere attraction, Murli was fast becoming something else, probably a good friend. But I was looking for something more, some kind of intimacy, and hoped he would satiate my undefined desires just like Sufal had done. Murli did not initiate any such advance, nor did I.

Yet, I hinted one evening in the most oblique manner talking to him about *The Naked Ape* and the phase I was in. He laughed and asked, *'Kya bol rahe hain aap* (What are you saying)?' To give my explanation some credibility, I spun a lie saying I had even consulted a doctor. He shrugged his shoulders, looked out of the window of the car and told me a story about his home town. Apparently, there were people like me who were suffering from a disease in the village he came from. He felt I could be cured by a priest or marriage, after having intercourse with 'my wife'—the person of the opposite sex that was now absent as *The Naked Ape* had said.

As the tenancy of the chummery ended, Murli also had to leave with his brother, even though he did not wish to. He wanted more time with me and had said so. A few days earlier, he had refused to cut his birthday cake until I returned home from work. The last hours were painful but there was no hugging or kissing like it had been with Sufal. I remember standing on the terrace looking down, seeing him leave. He turned back, waved, gave me a flying kiss, and left me with his vibrant smile saying, '*Phone karunga* (I will phone you).'

The timing of his departure could not have been worse as I had finally put in my papers at Penguin Books. I was alone at home, not occupied at all and kept waiting for him to call. His absence led me to do the strangest of things.

On several nights I sat in bed, waiting for something but I didn't know what. I would start to throw the pillows off the bed. Then I would pick up the magazines from the bedside and throw them too. On one night I spotted a film magazine that Murli liked which had Saif Ali Khan on the cover. He was one of his favourite actors and just a glimpse of that magazine left me agitated. I tore the cover to bits. Once the anger was over, it was tears that left my pillow wet.

I was longing for his naughtiness, the twinkle in his eyes, the ridiculous wrestling matches we enjoyed so much and the drives at night. I had disconnected the two-in-one in the kitchen as every time the radio played a song he liked I would remember him and feel even more miserable. I also discarded over a dozen cassettes I had bought for him. I didn't know what had come over me, I would often find myself staring at my reflection in the mirror in my toilet, trying to find an answer but I was blank.

Unlike Sufal, Murli wrote to me. It was the most surprising three-page letter I had ever received. He wrote in a mix of Hindi and English and in that letter while he used the words 'love' and 'missing you', he defined our friendship as one between two brothers, with me being his hero, a person he would never forget. This letter remained with me for years in an old file.

I never imagined seeing him again but as destiny would have it, we were to meet over a dozen years later in Mumbai. He was working as a cook with a family that owned a huge film production house. His sudden call was as surprising as my first sight of him. He was joyous as ever, '*Mere bhai, kaise ho* (Hey brother, how are you)?'

From the very slim innocent-looking boy, he had now turned into a stronger, muscular man, but he was as talkative as ever. He hadn't put on much height and had not lost the mischievous yet friendly smile that would reflect in his eyes too. He was married but living alone in Mumbai.

'*Bahut kuch bataana hai* (I have a lot to tell you)!' he said as we walked along the wall near the Gateway of India, ironically an area where men cruised men. He told me he liked the city, was now a good cook with a sense of multiple cuisines. What shocked me was his revelation that he swung from women to men, almost seamlessly—a bisexuality that didn't seem to bother him. He was just like Sufal, a person with an active libido and the love for lust. '*Main apne aapko rok nahin sakta* (I cannot stop myself),' he said rationalizing his infidelity, claiming that his love for his wife had never diminished. True, I would think, as his marriage remains intact and now has a child from it.

Chapter Eleven

WITH NO JOB in hand and a reluctance to find one, I spent most of my time in a youth association—Youth of Gulmohar—that Nitin and I had put together with other youngsters of our colony. From organizing events on environment, health and hygiene to creating platforms for talent contests and sports, we were a popular association in Gulmohar Park and neighbouring colonies. We also had a tabloid-size newsletter called *Expressions*, that I wrote and edited.

'You can't do this for the rest of your life,' Dilip said reminding me that four months had passed without a job. Sonu and Dilip spent a long evening at home discussing what it meant to work, earn and be responsible. Ma was present too but she said very little. I reiterated my desire to be a naturopath or maybe a teacher. Not giving either of these options even a moment of thought, journalism was thrown at me. The premise was that I liked to write and had been doing so in school, college and even now. 'There is a lot of respect and power attached to the pen,' Dilip said pitching the prospect.

'I do not want to be a reporter. I would rather have a desk job, probably editing copy,' I said. I did not like the idea of running around and meeting people all day long and I told them as much.

Still, I went to meet Paranjoy Guha Thakurta who was the then business editor of *The Pioneer*. This meeting was set up by Dilip who was then in the communications field working with a corporate.

The newspaper, although pretty small in terms of circulation, was highly respected given the team of journalists that worked there. I went through three rounds of interviews that focused on topics related to finance, stock markets and business. I had little to say and replied with basic knowledge on commerce and shares that I recalled from my class ten school textbook.

But somehow I was selected and started working at *The Pioneer*, in its business bureau. As a sub-cum-reporter, my profile entailed going out and meeting people related to the beats that had been allocated to me and report on those areas. Also, depending on the roster, I would have to stay on till late night to edit and place the reports on to a page as well.

I settled into this role of multitasking pretty quickly, writing my first feature for the Sunday edition of the paper within days of joining. It was on a topic I had little knowledge about—the NCAER (National Council of Applied Economic Research) report on consumption trends. I was soon writing on the Delhi Stock Exchange and then the Securities and Exchange Board of India. Even page-making, which had seemed so daunting earlier, was now not difficult as I was surrounded by a team that was helpful.

While I did bring some of my baking skills to the fore, sharing cookies and cakes every now and then, my record as a reporter stood out a lot more. This was in contrast to my stint at Penguin Books where no one recalled the work I did as it was below par for sure.

I was savouring my role with the newspaper. The appreciation from my colleagues, the calls from strangers wishing to meet me, the creation of a network of sources—all of it was changing who I was. When I attended a press conference, who I was mattered and not only to the organizers but to the reporters in other publications as well who were reading what I was reporting. I disliked missing news and felt elated while writing exclusives. I was just happy being in the office making a new set of acquaintances, not only in my bureau but across all the departments.

It was a general practice to read competing newspapers cover-to-cover to stay aware of one's competition. This meant scanning every page and not just the business section. This is when I came across a report that implied salaciousness of a different kind—men seeking men for sex. The article was about how such interactions took place in the dense and dark areas of Nehru Park, playing up homosexuality in a negative manner and alleging a sex racquet too.

I didn't have the wisdom then to see how a community had been profiled and displayed in a degrading and sensationalized manner. The only thing that mattered was there were other men like me. It was worth a try to see what Nehru Park was like, I thought, nervous and curious, driving down one Sunday evening.

As I reached one of the entry points on Vinay Marg, I saw just one other car in the parking area. The daylight was slowly fading and the area seemed desolate. I looked around feeling unsure of where I was and what lay ahead. I walked into the park surreptitiously as though I was going to steal something. It took me a few moments to adjust to the changing light. I saw silhouettes of trees and lamp posts bereft of electricity, at times even mistaking them for men.

It took me only ten minutes, which had seemed like hours, to spot one tall man. However, that triumphant moment turned into fright as he moved his eyes in the direction I was. I felt intimidated, unsafe, exposed and scared. He was about six feet in height and muscular enough to be a bouncer.

As he started to move towards me, I felt a desperate anxiety to leave. I moved quickly to the gate I had entered from. I rushed to the car and drove out of the parking lot hurriedly. I was panting and my heart was beating fast. I drove with no destination in mind for around half an hour before deciding to return home.

I rushed to my room, pulled out the news report and read it again to see if I had missed anything the first time. I am not sure whether I was fearful, angry or upset, but I tore the report into shreds. That day, I was sure I would never return to Nehru Park, at least not for the purpose of finding a man. I was also certain that 'cruising' to find another man—a stranger—in a dark, public space, was not something that I had the courage for.

Chapter Twelve

A LITTLE OVER a year into journalism, I had offers coming my way from competing publications, business newspapers and magazines. I was caught between my emotions and commitment towards a small team and my career growth and a larger platform. I also felt a certain allegiance towards people like Paranjoy and my editor, A. K. Bhattacharya (AKB).

However, with rumours circulating that Paranjoy was quitting—which he eventually did—and that AKB was considering returning to a business daily, I thought it was best to consider moving out too. This is when I decided to join *The Economic Times*.

1 January 1996 was the first day at my new job. I noticed that the two bureaus of economic and corporate here were probably larger than three departments put together in *The Pioneer*. The greatness in numbers and the vastness of the floor area was overwhelming in itself.

The only way for me to settle down was to file reports which I did on day one, hitting the front page. I don't know what exactly drove me—maybe it was seeing my name in print or the desire to excel or to live up to my father's name. I know the latter did create its own pressure as there were certain expectations built around Pa's legacy. I had colleagues, who were close to retirement, recalling their first days in journalism, a time when they met Pa, who they admired. Even at *The Pioneer*, if I was on a run of exclusive reports, it was attributed to my genes.

In a year or so, I was writing special reports for the Sunday edition of the paper as well as a music column. I went on to break scams and even did a bit of investigative journalism exposing certain airlines, their ownership patterns and so on. I received threats at times and it wasn't unusual for certain corporations to try and silence us journalists by offering favours or underhand deals, none of which were ever entertained by me.

By the last quarter of 1997, I had moved into the economic bureau following a discomfiture with corporate reporting. This is the time when I came under the leadership of M. K. Venu. He was one of the friendliest persons across all the bureaus. He was easy to get along with and a great thinker. Venu's idea of reporting was not merely about breaking stories and being ahead of others, it meant to put a context to a news development and see the big picture.

I also got to know Venu's wife, Chitra. The clarity of her mind was reflected in the crispness of her voice, her friendly eyes and warm smile. She was the one who usually picked up the phone when I called Venu every morning around 7.30 after reading the newspapers. In time, she started reading me well; she couldn't read my mind, but she could correctly interpret my tone and general mood.

There was an intimacy in this bureau. We hung out together and Venu, on many occasions, had hosted us at his home. Some of my other colleagues also organized dinners at their residence and I did so too. As a result, the personal and professional did blur at times.

This environment made working far more conducive to productivity. I was covering several beats, collaborating with other reporters and was soon called a 'star' reporter by many, including Venu. I remember a senior edit team head saying I was making my father proud. That was the most gratifying statement I had ever heard.

Between the end of 1997 and December 1998, a period of

approximately twelve months, I was set to receive my second promotion. I also got a significant salary hike of close to 20 per cent. These developments brought a lot of focus on me. Suddenly, I was a freshly pressed principal correspondent at the age of twenty-nine—this pushed me straight into the marriage market as an eligible bachelor.

'I have a friend, Samrita. She is single. She will be in Delhi in a couple of weeks, why don't you meet her?' asked Pratibha, a colleague of mine.

Pratibha was not just a beautiful woman but a strong individual with a mind of her own. Her sense of self and her open acceptance of the modern Anglicized world—more often referred to as Western culture—made her stand out from the crowd. Yet, all of this 'modernity' contrasted with her immediate agenda to set me up on a date, not only because I needed to 'settle down' but also because my 'mother needed someone around'.

I had never given marriage a serious thought even though a few relatives and friends would ask me or Ma, on when I'd tie the knot. Ma would usually respond saying that just like Dilip and Duji, it was for me to decide. My answer was always yes, with a rider that I had to earn more to sustain a marriage.

At that point, however, I was hoping Samrita could be the answer or the beacon to lead me out of my 'homosexual' phase and towards a normal life. This became the reason for me to say yes to Pratibha.

Samrita arrived in Delhi for a short trip. She was slightly younger than me, but seemed a lot more sure and confident than I was. An engineer by profession, she made it known that moving to Delhi would not be a difficult task. 'I would get a job easily,' she said, emphasizing her preparedness. She was neither thin nor stout—somewhere in the middle I would say.

It was a pleasant meeting of easy conversations, something I had become adept at being a journalist. There wasn't any excitement or a high though as there were casual, polite conversations ranging from the weather to the work we did.

After that first meeting, Pratibha took charge of my 'dating' life. She decided every step I was to take, how often I should meet, when to visit Samrita and even set up the pace on phone calls I was to make. 'You know nothing about dating,' she had said and that was true. I followed her every direction to the T and seemed 'bereft of emotions'—an observation made by two of my colleagues.

It was a tumultuous period of ups and downs, routine, stress, dilemmas and a continuous engagement with Samrita. When she made her first visit to my home, to reassure herself of my background, I was having the worst morning that I could remember. It started with a dizzy spell that did not allow me out of bed for a long time, leading me to call in sick at work. Venu felt it was an anxiety attack implying I was under pressure about Samrita's impending visit home. Ma said I had been restless most of the night as I turned and twisted, and even mumbled in my sleep, lying on the mattress on the floor in her room.

I wasn't sure what it was.

Every time I tried to get up, I felt like I was in a whirlpool, everything would start going round in circles and I would lose my balance and fall back flat on the mattress. My nape was hurting and the nerves seemed stressed. I felt disoriented. It took me a few hours before I felt sure enough to be on my feet and meet Samrita.

That one visit, however, 'reassured' her of whatever she needed to know and led to the addition of one more task in my daily routine—calls to her as directed by Pratibha. These phone calls, which never seemed to stimulate my mind or get me excited in any manner whatsoever, took the relationship to another level (as Pratibha saw it)—visiting her at her home in Lucknow.

Ma was predictably happy. I, on the other hand, was merely going through the motions. I reached the town early morning, on a Friday, with a plan to spend all day with Samrita. I reached her house and met with her mother and sister who were warm and welcoming and made me feel comfortable. Soon enough, both of them disappeared, almost suddenly, leaving me and Samrita alone. After lunch, we went out in her car. 'There is a spot I want to take you to. It is where lovers go,' Samrita said. The drive was breathtakingly beautiful and I would have enjoyed the vistas a lot more if it were not for a hand that lay on my hand. My body got rigid and every bit of me seemed to shrink with a desperate need to escape that moment and maybe even jump out of the car.

I couldn't fathom why, her every action made me freeze. I think I visibly cringed and she noticed it. She quickly moved her hand away. She took the car off the road and swerved it to the right, parking it next to a cafe. I hurriedly got out of the car. Looking around and noticing that we were not alone any more, I heaved a sigh of relief. Till then, I was not even aware of the many beads of sweat that had been steadily trickling down my brows and sideburns.

'We can go back to my home if you like,' she said in a tone that almost insisted that this was the option she sought. I felt a sense of fear. I think my blood pressure had dropped.

'I think we should be heading back to the station now,' I looked at my watch pointedly, trying to remind her of what time it was. The rest of the journey passed without any incident and any kind of a conversation. We reached the station just in time—there were less than ten minutes left for the train to leave. I bid her a stoic goodbye and went and sat in the train, utterly exhausted and a bit dazed, not knowing exactly what had happened.

But I knew I felt relieved—why I felt so, I did not know.

Chapter Thirteen

WITHIN A DAY of my return, the wheels of courtship started moving really quickly. Our daily casual conversations over the phone suddenly got serious. Samrita wanted to get engaged, cementing the several weeks of interaction, and even said that we could not speak or meet unless this formality was completed.

I was taken off guard not knowing whether things were moving too fast or in the right direction. I literally went with the flow not thinking of anything and responding in the same manner as I had done when Pratibha first sought to introduce us to each other. The only thing I did was buy time saying I needed to discuss the matter with Ma who left it to me, adding she had no objection.

As 11 April was fixed for the engagement, a few days after my cousin, Purabi's wedding the symptoms of stress or anxiety—as Venu put it—returned to haunt me every now and then. However, the sense of celebration at home and in the bureau influenced my mood which improved briefly as I went about finding an engagement ring. I had never realized before how much I enjoyed looking at the designs of necklaces and earrings and the variety of jewellery-related accessories that women indulged in. We rummaged through several design books, screened some thirty trays of rings in silver and gold before I finally found something that I thought was beautiful. 'I have rarely seen a man spend so much time trying to pick a ring. You must really love her,' the store owner said.

I had this urge to speak to someone to share the near finality of this new chapter of my life. I called up Moushumi, my classmate from FAPS. 'That is good news, Sharif. I did not expect to hear this from you.' She giggled over the phone. 'So are you in love?' I paused for a few seconds and said that I would eventually fall in love. 'Isn't that how it is?' I asked.

Her world view of life and love was absolutely different from mine. She felt that any relationship, and definitely marriage, required passion and love from the beginning. 'You need to be attracted to Samrita. I don't get that feeling from you when you talk about her,' she said in her typical nonchalant manner. Moushumi's candidness left me with murmurs in my head.

I thought the best thing to do at that moment was to put pen to paper and weigh the pros and cons of my situation. It was evident I was not attracted to Samrita. It was also clear that while I froze at her touch, I had welcomed the advances made by Sufal and was even keen to sleep with Murli. From the time I had met her till now, while I had had no physical interaction with any man, my eyes had not stopped roving—something I expected would have happened if Samrita and I got together.

On the other hand, I knew she wasn't ugly and I found other women attractive too. There were so many relationships that I knew of which never began over a sexual encounter. Maybe if Samrita and I were under the same roof, the relationship would ease into a strong and happy marriage. What worried me, in addition, was whether I would become like Sufal or a Murli, having clandestine affairs with men on the side. This was a question that drained a fair bit of energy out of me.

After several hours spent scribbling on pieces of paper, the impending engagement with Samrita outweighed my doubts.

From Uma masi to Duji, everyone had flown in. The whole family was on a high of sorts, planning a new room for me—the third bedroom in our home—on one of the terraces that lay on the side of the dining and living rooms. Talks of upgrading the kitchen were also going on. My career too came into focus with everyone wondering when I would become an editor.

By around 4 in the afternoon of 11 April, as I was getting ready for the engagement, Ma came frantically into the room Duji and I were sharing. Apparently, the plans had changed. Samrita's uncle had called to say that the engagement needed to be put on hold but they would continue to host us for tea. Ma looked bewildered and Duji said, 'This is strange!'

What unfolded was an hour of peculiar twists and turns with everyone eventually leaving the final decision on what we should do, entirely on me! I looked at Duji hoping he would give me an answer. 'It is your life, not anyone else's,' he told me simply.

I decided to speak with Samrita, as suggested by Ma, and took my call within seconds. 'My grandmother wants us to hold the engagement later,' she said. 'But why?' I asked. 'She feels the engagement and wedding can be held together but it is best that the two families meet as planned,' she said everything could be sorted out during the meeting. I insisted that I needed to have more details before I spoke to Ma and the rest of my family. This is when her uncle called and spoke a bit forcefully, explaining nothing, not why they first suggested an engagement and then cancelled it and turned the whole event into a high-tea function.

Even Samrita had no answer.

I don't know what came over me. I changed from a meek follower to a more decisive person. I posed the questions, and did not wait for Pratibha or anyone else to dictate the script. Ultimately, I put my foot down and pulled out of the engagement as well as the function in the evening. I told a sobbing Samrita, 'This exchange of rings is not merely symbolic; it is an engagement where trust and faith are the basis of things. This is not a birthday party where someone forgot to bring the cake.'

Even as she did not reveal what was brewing in her family, she said plainly, 'Ignore them. This marriage is about us and not them.' Yet, I flatly declined, being self-righteous and portraying values that families and society generally blindly thrived on. I told her, 'We lack trust here, let's just admit that. My family is being treated with no respect. However independent we may be, we do marry into families which is why you came home too.'

There was a newfound crispness in all I was saying and doing. I felt relief, a sense of independence, much like a bird let out of its cage for the first time. I didn't even want to ponder over the past few hours. I guess if there had been any furrows on my forehead due to stress or tension, they must have disappeared.

From family to friends, everyone was proud of how I acted, concerned about my feelings and critical of Samrita's family.

What they didn't know was that it had been me who had rushed out of this 'engagement' even when I knew that Samrita was ready to sit in my car and exchange rings without the blessings of her loved ones. I am sure even Ma would have accepted this arrangement but I still chose to close that door.

I wondered then, and sometimes even now, how Samrita would recall the events of that day. Would she blame her family or me or even Pratibha? Or would she have blamed circumstances or destiny?

Whether it was destiny or divine intervention, I was grateful and indebted to those moments that transformed my life in a manner I had never foreseen!

Chapter Fourteen

I WAS IN office the very next day, although relatives and colleagues had suggested that I take some time off to recover from the unexpected 'disengagement'. But I loved my job and was enjoying it like before.

At home, as planned, construction of the new room and the upgradation of the kitchen had started that very month. Even if there wasn't a Samrita, there was bound to be another girl in my life later, so the room had to be constructed.

Mid-summer was usually a lean period for our bureau that primarily covered government departments, ministries and public policies. And, as expected, news flow had dropped. Thus, this was the time when we had a lot more conversations on topics that were not connected to work. They included films, music, family matters, food and cuisines, sports, to name a few.

I recall returning from a meeting with a source to find that a few of my colleagues—mostly women—were animatedly discussing a documentary film called *Summer in My Veins*—a film that I did see months later. At that point though, the documentary was being shown at several film festivals in the country including at some event at Delhi's India Habitat Centre. My ears perked up when I heard the word homosexual. I also heard another term—coming out.

I sat in my cubicle picking up all that was being said about the film. It was made by a young filmmaker, Nishit Saran, who in this short film tells his mother he is gay, holding a camera that is focused on her for most of the time. My colleagues had mixed views on his sexuality and how the film was made. Some said that it was over-dramatized, while some others said such stories were necessary, but all of them claimed that it was not uncommon to find gay men.

There were a few who felt it was weird to be homosexual and considered it a mental disorder but some of them veered towards it being a sexual choice and just how some people were. 'I think there are bisexual people, married men sleeping with other men,' said one of my colleagues who quoted from Indian scriptures and her own interactions with gay men. The counter was that men had uncontrollable libido and so they could have sex with anyone or anything, man to man was just circumstantial.

The name of a former journalist also popped up—Ashok Row Kavi. While one of my colleagues got up and left saying being gay was not normal, the ones still engaging in the conversation called him brave and admirable having come out in the 1980s. As I diarized this, it seemed being a homosexual or gay was not necessarily a 'phase'. There were differing views on the subject but there were a Kavi and a Saran too, who had declared they were homosexuals

This is when the benefits of coming early to office, much before the others, around 10 a.m., were reaped. I had a computer to myself, did not have to share it and could use the internet freely. I logged into Yahoo and Excite—two of the search engines those days. None of them, of course, were accessed regularly as they did not function like Google does today. The web itself at that time was more about emails replacing snail mail (regular post) than information surfing.

Still, I keyed in the names I had noted as well as the term, homosexuality. I found out about Saran—a handful of reports. He was termed 'courageous' to have shot such a film and risked his standing in society by openly saying he was gay. There was criticism too and several reports suggesting people like him had a mental disorder and required help. I also read about Kavi and the backlash he faced when he spoke about his sexuality to the press, recording it in Indian history, as such.

The information on homosexuality was more about definitions and the history of the word which came into being in the late nineteenth century. I found next to nothing about it either being a phase or the normal path of life, that is, the co-existence of homosexuality and heterosexuality, one leading to another. There were reports about homosexuality being a sin and even illegal in India. This, of course, scared me.

Still, my curiosity at that moment pushed me further and I started looking for more information using the phrases—'men having sex with men', 'men lusting for men' and 'male intimacy with men'. I kept searching and found bits and pieces of information that were hateful of homosexuals, describing them as effeminate, loud, retarded and strange.

I recall looking at myself, wondering if I fitted the profile sufficiently of being a gay man I wasn't colourful or effeminate. The vision I had of myself was neither macho nor woman-like. No one had ever called me pansy, girly or sissy (terms that stuck in my head reading them in the few articles found online)—though I had once been called sissy but that was a long time ago.

My mind was in a muddle, not knowing what to accept as the truth. Unlike past dilemmas though, I was not stressed. On the contrary, I was eager to find out more. I also went to the office library and tried to find write-ups on Kavi and Saran unsure whether the web had enough verified information. It was a tedious task as there was no specific category identifiable to locate such information. And there was no way I could ask the librarian for help, not with all the criticism and hate I found attached to homosexuality. He might think I was gay and gossip about me.

I finally gave up my search in the huge library, as I did not know where to look. That is when it struck me that Venu knew Kavi and might have his number, which I found later in his telephone diary, literally stealing it from there.

Chapter Fifteen

AS LUCK WOULD have it, the new room at my home was more or less ready with the roof laid and only some finishing work left. It was around that time when my cousin, Bijoya, who lived in Mumbai, called me over to take a break with her at her home. I could not say no!

On reaching Mumbai, that wet July, I spent most of my time with her shopping, cooking and staying up gabbing almost every night. As much as I enjoyed my time with her, at the back of my mind was always the call I had to make.

I often looked longingly at the slip of paper that had Kavi's phone number but could never muster up enough courage to dial it. I hesitated for days, and also feared that my cousin would overhear my conversation with a well-known and an openly gay man.

My thoughts scaled daunting heights of unreality—how could I risk letting the 'secret' out? I feared being shamed as speaking about sex and sexual attraction, in any case, was not a done thing; and who had ever talked about men being attracted to other men.

Days passed and I lost count of the phone booths along the streets of Colaba to Fort in South Mumbai I had stared at hesitatingly assuming they would come alive and give away the conversation I wished to have. I recall walking in once, surveying the surroundings, looking at the many people waiting, some eyes meeting and others urging me to get done with the call even as I did not dial the number. On two occasions, I did dial in, heard the ring, put the coin in the slot but hung up once the call was received.

Soon eight days of the ten-day holiday had passed. I made another attempt. I walked in after waiting in an unusually long line, took a deep breath and dialled the number again. This time I did not put down the phone back in the cradle. Kavi was at the other end of the line. 'This is Sharif here. I am a journalist based in Delhi and needed help, I am...' I didn't have to say anything else as Kavi immediately recognized my circumstances.

Every Saturday, he told me, gay men met, to my amazement, in Delhi's Gulmohar Park—the same colony I resided in! The meetings were hosted by Anjali Gopalan's Naz Foundation under a programme called Humrahi. 'Have you interacted with any other gay men?' Kavi asked like it was some normal courtesy. He was the first one I was talking to, not sure if Sufal or Murli counted as gay. So, I answered in the negative.

'It may be worth your while to meet some from the community in Mumbai. There are regular meetings held at a cafe in Bandra and if I am not wrong, there is one tomorrow as well. You are most welcome to attend,' he said. I hesitated indicating I was unsure of myself but Kavi, in an abrupt manner, said, 'No one is asking you to have sex or even go on a date. You would just be meeting other people like you, that is all. Otherwise I would have told you to go to the dark Voodoo bar or walk along the wall near Radio Club'.

For Kavi, saying things plainly was normal. It was he who had first come out in *Savvy* magazine as early as 1986. He had even started *Bombay Dost*—a magazine I came to know of only around that time. For him, I learnt, everything was normal. Hate was normal, the struggle was a reality, to speak up was not unusual and to have sex was natural. I learnt later that he had spent over a decade building a safety net of sorts for the gay community. He started the Humsafar Trust that is arguably one of the most impactful NGOs in the areas of HIV/AIDS and queer issues.

'It isn't unusual for people like you to meet at a designated cafe to mingle with others like yourself. While some would stay on to chit-chat, others would go to a party at a dingy bar or private space. Many would even explore their sexuality,' Kavi said matter-of-factly, conjuring in me fear of sexual inexperience and the reality that people slept around easily. My inhibitions got the better of me and I spent the evening with Bijoya.

Within two days of this conversation, I was riding back home on the *August Kranti Rajdhani Express*. I was excited, unsure, anxious, and all this nervous energy mixed with trepidation took away my sleep throughout the sixteen-hour journey. I reached on a Sunday morning. This gave Ma and me a long day to chat about my trip to Mumbai. I told her about the shopping expeditions, the food and the beautiful old home that Bijoya lived in.

Ma, with her keen observation, said I was unusually excited. The last time she saw me in a similar state of mind, refreshed and relaxed, was after my holiday in Kolkata when I was in school. She was obviously unaware of the reasons for my elation then or now. I could never have told her why, not just yet.

That night I sat in my room, took out the slip of paper with the email address of the programme head of Humrahi and copied it in my reporter's pad. The next day, I reached work early. I quietly walked towards a corner terminal that was half enclosed. This was a dingy part of the news bureau and far more private. I turned on the computer, opened my Hotmail account and started writing a short email to the programme head.

The meetings, as per the reply, usually started around 6 in the evening ending anywhere between 8.30 and 9 p.m. There was no dress code or restriction on what one wore except for this subtle directive: 'please keep in mind that this is a residential area and one should not wear anything that disturbs the sentiments of the people in the vicinity'.

Chapter Sixteen

ALMOST FOUR WEEKS went by and I had still not been to any Humrahi meeting. At one level, I was sceptical, unsure of what to expect and wondered what happened at such meetings. At another, I feared that my neighbours would spot me entering the premises of Naz Foundation—which was hardly five minutes away from my home.

Duji and his wife, Peggy, were also visiting at that time and every Saturday was spent with them, hanging out at a bar, meeting relatives or in just some unplanned activity. I knew, though, that they would never have had a problem if I had plans of my own. But they would have been curious and I would have to think up a story, not knowing that lying was to become a habit, just weeks from then.

The two of them left early in the week of 9 August, which freed the coming Saturday for me to go to the meeting. Preparing for the meeting and attempting to overcome my nerves, I decided to head to the D block property which turned out to be a nondescript two-storey house. I surveyed the surroundings like a criminal would do of a proposed crime scene. I measured the distance up to the gate, looked at the ground floor, saw the small garden in front and scanned the stairs going up to the first floor.

Nothing looked unusual. There were no giveaways or even a hint of men or anyone who seemed to look different around the building. I actually didn't know what I was looking for or what different meant, but I just searched to find something that was distinct. After a couple of more such visits, the only takeaway was that I found the ideal parking spot.

Saturday finally arrived. I had never given Saturdays much importance until now. I was a home boy and if I ever stepped out on a Saturday it was to attend a family function, a press event or just to saunter the by-lanes of the colony. Ma was also always in the loop, she knew all my colleagues and friends. While this, in itself, was a reflection of how involved she was in my life, it also posed a challenge—where was I going to be that evening, what time would I return and who would I be with? She never asked these questions but so far I had never hidden any such information from her.

A moment of creativity came over to save me. As I was to represent India later that year at a WIPO (World Intellectual Property Organization) conference in Geneva on a topic such as intellectual property, a complex subject, I told Ma there was a series of skill-enhancement workshops I had to attend on Saturday evenings. I wasn't sure what time they'd get over and assumed it might not be before 10 p.m. which meant I would be home half an hour later.

Ma, fortunately, bought this story.

I rushed home by 5 p.m., showered quickly, sprayed the only cologne I owned and stood in front of the cupboard to pick out a shirt. Normally, I spent less than five minutes selecting a shirt and a matching pair of pants. I often wore long Fabindia or Khadi Gramodyog kurtas—again something that I just randomly picked off the hangers in my cupboard. But this evening was different.

I picked a red-brick-coloured shirt and then placed it back. I took out a black and white-striped shirt, and returned it to its hanger. I then started to look for the brightest shirt I had because I believed gay men wore bright clothes as this was what I had read in a couple of articles online. This is also what the ladies in my bureau had said during the conversation I had overheard earlier that summer.

The brightest and probably the most striking in my collection was a near-psychedelic blue, Chinese collared shirt. Exhausted with the process of selection, I wore it with a pair of carbon blue jeans and sports shoes. 'Isn't that a bit bright for a workshop?' Ma asked as I was stepping out. 'I just want to look different for a change,' I said with a smile.

As a part of my cover-up and to maintain the sanctity of my story, I took my car even though I was going to be in the colony. I drove in and was near the Naz Foundation office in less than two minutes. I knew exactly where to park but sat in my car for a long while not sure whether I wished to step out and walk towards that building.

I was so scared that I felt threatened even by the trees!

I kept the engine running and moved the car up and down a few inches pretending that I was trying to park in the most perfect way. Every time I saw someone walk by, I would look away in the other direction, trying to hide my face. I was not only wary of my neighbours, but was also conscious of the Gopalan family who lived in the ground floor of the building. They were known to Ma and could tell her that they saw me. If this wasn't a worry I wondered if I would fit in the group. From realistic concerns, I travelled to the most wild—the fear of contracting a sexually transmitted disease—not knowing then how absurd and ill-informed I was.

I rested my head on the steering wheel and it was a bit calming. I was breathing more easily. I told myself that if not today, I would have to come back next Saturday as there was no turning back on entering that office and meeting the people there. I could decide never to return but I had to go in first, I convinced myself.

I squeezed myself through the partially open iron gate, happy that the space was just enough for my frame to go through, ensuring there were no squeaky sounds that might catch the attention of anyone around. Therefore, with almost no chance of being spotted I rushed past the ground floor door and scampered up to reach the first floor.

Outside the room lay over twenty pairs of shoes and slippers. So, I removed my shoes too, reached for the door handle and gently, very slowly, pulled it down and pushed the door open. My head was in first and then came the rest of me. What I saw were many eyes turning towards me—it was a collective glare that was neither positive nor negative. I felt I was on stage for the first time, suffering from stage fright, a fish literally out of water.

There were a few words, whispers and murmurs, none of which I could pick up but I knew I was suddenly a topic of discussion amongst those who had noticed my entry. A representative from Naz Foundation, Rajeev, came up to me, asked my name and said he had been informed about me—a newcomer. 'Have you been counselled?' he asked. I was not aware of any such requirement or that there was a pre-meeting process. 'Don't worry,' he said, guiding me to a spot amongst the group that was now a circular-shaped gathering of men and boys.

I settled in within minutes and the eyes that seemed to have been glaring at me earlier didn't seem so frightening any more. I had a Bengali intellectual on my left named Polash, who was a university teacher, and a young Assamese boy who had just entered, on my right. As it turned out, I was the only journalist in that group and being so had its own merits in the eyes of students and professors from universities. There was, of course, a certain profiling and assumption that I would talk on topics that they found engaging—current affairs, corruption and capitalism—unlike certain other gay men who were inclined more towards fashion, design and the fine arts.

While Polash and I chatted, my mind was still on Dheeman. I kept turning to look at him. He was wearing a deep green short kurta and off-white trousers that were usually called chinos. He was a little over five feet tall, skinny, with beautiful chestnut-brown eyes. He was someone who knew music and listened to the same bands and solo artists that I had grown up with. He knew of Pink Floyd, the Rolling Stones, Bob Dylan and Led Zeppelin. He was also aware of the sultry-styled protest of Nina Simone and the joyous warmth of Etta James. They were all treasured and loved enough by me to be impressed with anyone who knew them.

The twinkle in his eyes as he spoke about them was charming and attractive. His diction was appealing too—it was crisp and certain. He lived very close to my home—in the Asian Games Village Complex adjacent to the Siri Fort Auditorium. This I guess could be defined as a 'marriage of convenience' (if it were to happen), so easy to reach and so much music to share.

However, my inability to cut short a conversation with Polash meant I hardly got time to have a long conversation with Dheeman—who was my first-ever 'gay' crush. In fact, I didn't even see him leave, missing the chance to walk down the stairs and chat with him after the meeting concluded.

Still, as his absence left me sullen, the Humrahi meeting was a new chapter of my life.

Each of us introduced ourselves, many used aliases or nicknames—a practice that protected one's identity, a fact that I got to know only weeks later. This was the kind of information a counselling session would have provided me with. I, of course, shared my name as it was. I also talked about the place I worked at and shared my business card too—another no-no in the community.

I went on to provide the location and address of my home to a few of them. Again, it was only later that I learnt that such information was given only if you wanted to invite someone to your bedroom to have sex. Effectively, I may have misled quite a few men that evening into believing I fancied them and was looking for some mating. With no follow-ups and the fact that my address was now with several men (and word got around quickly in that group), I may have got them to believe that I was slippery, a slut and someone who indulged in group sex.

Putting these errors of judgement and ignorance aside, I did learn a fair bit in those two hours. Many feared that their names would go out into the large cruel world of hate. Trust was so low that one could not even rely on one's own community. Even talking about your place of work had its risks as loose conversations could out a person, destroy a career and even take away the roof over one's head.

If there was something I held back, it was my mobile number only because telecom companies levied a charge of over ₹16 per minute for incoming calls. The home phone number, though, was given to a few!

Rajeev saw me passing my business card I think and told me to be judicious. 'This is not a group of journalists at a press conference,' he told me, drawing the line. He offered to 'protect' and guide me through this new world. In return, I was to help him put together some kind of media list that Naz Foundation could target to help propagate and support what had become 'my' community in that little time.

I felt so comfortable and grateful by the end of the meeting that I, without hesitation, placed a few hundred of rupees in the hat that went around to cover the costs of hosting it. There were comments on my contribution as I was viewed as privileged, not necessarily by education but by the address I had, the certainty of a job and the power that journalists were assumed to have.

Rajeev told me that very few people in the meeting had permanent jobs or job security as such. Many had left their homes to live in Delhi and make a life for themselves. Some gay men had family businesses but only a few could carry that forward usually diluting their sexuality to fit in to the family structure. If they, or anyone for that matter, had to start out on their own, it was a huge struggle as Delhi was a city of networks that weren't easy to crack.

There were many who struggled through school or college for the lack of any support structure and the silent oppression of a stereotypical world. 'Quite a few drop out,' he informed me as the teasing, bullying and violence pushed many to the brink.

Given that background, I asked Rajeev whether my contribution was patronizing in nature or offensive. I told him that I was just very thankful for the space we had. He dismissed my thoughts and told me not to overanalyse.

In the weeks to come, I met so many regulars and a few new people too. Discussions veered from stories of abuse and violence to love in general and even sex within and outside a relationship. There were even doctors coming in who educated us about safe sex. I remember how scared we were once when we got to know that diseases could be sexually transmitted, and we weren't only talking about HIV and AIDS. These were sexually transmitted infections or STIs as they are commonly called now. I believe that night just about everyone dropped the idea of a one-night stand. I was petrified even to kiss someone, not that I had kissed anyone since Sufal!

We also had film viewing sessions besides conversations with activists from other cities. At times, we celebrated a festival with contributions of money, food and soft drinks. It was then that I first met Anjali Gopalan—the lady behind Naz Foundation.

She was revered, loved and was a pillar of support to many. Over the years, I got to know how she had stood strongly against the hostility that some residents in the colony had shown. She fought the police on many occasions, protecting strangers of our community. She even gave mentally ill men and women shelter in her home, none of which has changed even today.

I remember my first conversation with her. It was a short one. I introduced myself and she immediately asked, 'Rangnekar? A block? How is Veena?' She knew who I was and that got me worried as I assumed she would tell Ma we had met here. Or her parents would talk of my presence at Humrahi. But my fears were misplaced. Soon I realized her parents were completely aware of what her Foundation did and that the identity of anyone who visited the first floor of their home was to be kept confidential. 'Convey my wishes to your mom or don't—depends on whether she knows you are here,' Anjali said, leaving things to me.

There was obviously a lot of secrecy within that space. Even though Ma had been to her home on the ground floor, she had never known of Naz Foundation and the Humrahi group. Anjali's parents, I learnt, had never provided an elaborate description of the work that the Foundation did even though they were proud of their daughter's courage.

Weeks into the meetings, I was asked if I had met the love of my life or had I slept with anyone yet. I had nothing to say which came as a surprise to the group that had been discussing their sex life, pretty much in the same nonchalant manner as my brothers used to chat about their encounters with women. As our group of six expanded to eight or nine people, the debate shifted gears moving into the arena of open relationships and what commitment meant.

It was completely clear that there was more than one camp in this regard. A commitment, to the majority, meant a promise between two lovers that love and physical intimacy such as sex was only within the boundaries of that commitment.

At the same time, a small yet vocal section said we needed to come out of the structures that society at large believed in. 'We need our own paths, our ideas of romance need not be adopted from a Hollywood or Bollywood film. What a family is should not be a template handed down from generation to generation,' one of them said. A commitment should be left for an individual or couples to determine and not dictated by the normative or what was later referred to as the hetero-normative, influencing how we thought and lived.

What happens to love then, who is that special person you

want to be with when you grow old, breathing your last asked a few. I remember one of the men who had returned from Canada felt that the idea of one-night stands itself destroyed the idea of love. 'The more you sleep around, the greater is the chance to erode the emotions attached to intimacy and making love,' he had contended. He went on to suggest that making love was too precious to be given out freely, denying it any sanctity.

The counter was simple—to distinguish love from sex. The latter is purely physical—just sex. The former is a mix of emotions and sex and what is essentially love-making. The easiest way out was taking neither side, and just say 'to each his own'.

It was a lot for me to digest. I kept my mouth shut since I feared being called out as foolish as I had no experience to base my views on. However, I did tend to lean towards what was being called a conservative view—love and having sex were both closely linked and a part of a relationship and a commitment.

And the truth was that at that point in time I was seeking intimacy and love as a singular package, not one distinct from the other.

Chapter Seventeen

LIFE, AS IT was destined to be, was changing and how. In a couple of weeks, telling lies to Ma about my whereabouts on Saturday evenings became so easy that I now had, what one could call, a parallel life—one that was private and a secret, while the other for Ma and the world around me.

Even though Saturday evenings were precious and I did not wish to miss any of them, particularly the outings that followed, I was also hanging out with Rajeev and a few new friends I met at Humrahi such as Adi—who I had started talking to very often—and a group of interior designers, architects, art collectors and software professionals. I had a rapport with Subhashish Mandal who was building a career in architecture and now is a noted blogger too, and Dhirendra, who was a software engineer, working from home.

I was the first person entering their circle in over a year. Oddly, I had little to offer in terms of conversations as it often revolved around men or design or the designs they had on certain men. Each one of them worked independently, clearly unsure whether they would fit into a structured environment dominated by heterosexual men. The talk amongst men in workplaces was often about women, and something you were expected to participate in. At times, the humour revolved around masculinity and jokes abounded at the expense of the gay community. That was something even I had experienced at work. 'There is no space for our kind of conversation, not even with women,' I had heard some of them say.

One big struggle most of us had was regarding our social lives—the weekend in particular. It was assumed that if there were an office group heading out somewhere, we would bring 'our girl' along. If we did not have a girlfriend, our colleagues—with no bad intent—often tried to set us up or match-make, of course, with a girl. In such social gatherings, discussions usually veered towards games like cricket or football, none of which were particularly popular or interesting for a large number of gay men, at least in urban Delhi.

'They have little to do with us,' Dhirendra told me, admiring how I continued to enjoy my work at *The Economic Times*.

Dhirendra was the more subdued one in the group. He was from Pune and had settled in Delhi to create a life of his own building on his skills as a graphic designer, moving into software development and so on. He had large eyes, a clear diction and loved literature which showed in his language. Books were his best friends followed by photography, he had once told me. It was Dhirendra who pulled me into this group. He had a view on everything from politics to arts and would converse with me in a manner that showed he wanted to know more about who I was, or maybe he was just helping me to get to know myself. We took long walks in the lawns beside India Gate. We sipped coffee on and off and even planned outings to gay parties.

This group was partially responsible for making an attempt to create a Friday gathering at a bar in New Friends Colony. We would grab a table in the corner and then add a few more to accommodate around fifteen or twenty of us. The fact that we could not get more than around ten to a dozen of us to be there was indicative of how difficult it was for many to be a 'gay man' out in the public. As we expected, although we hoped not, this effort whittled away in weeks.

I remember once I was heading back from the gathering with Dhirendra, dropping him off at his single-room home in Jangpura.

We sat in the car for quite a while. I told him about developments at work and the WIPO conference in Geneva where I was headed too later in November. He spoke about his new technology skills and client sign-ups that he had made which I absorbed in awe. It was past midnight when all of a sudden, his fingers touched one of my ears. He was rubbing it gently as he adjusted himself on the seat to face me. I was surprised and felt repulsed.

'Loosen up, Sharif,' Dhirendra politely urged me and then brought his face in front of my face, placed his lips on mine, trying to force a kiss. I pushed him away and said sorry, 'It is best you leave Dhirendra, I am not looking for this from you.'

He was visibly surprised. Staring out through the window, Dhirendra believed I was aware that every action of his, be it spending time with me, the coffee 'dates', the conversations and parties, had been indicative of his interest in me. 'But I never looked at you that way. I thought of you as a friend,' I said in a slightly embarrassed manner.

I soon dropped off from that group remaining in touch with only a person or two but rarely joining them. In any case, I had to spend time with Rajeev who was keen I help him build a media plan. He and I usually met over coffee. I would carry sheaves of papers with details on reporters and feature writers. Rajeev believed it was important for me to understand the community a lot better and that was by starting with myself. If not myself, I should at least know more about him, before we embarked on developing a media strategy.

A couple of coffee sessions went by with Rajeev sharing his story—an admirable one, indeed. He had come out at his home and was probably among the better counsellors that Humrahi had. He was also a brilliant writer, working with a publishing house. He thought my short tenure with Penguin Books was a special connection with him, exclaiming 'no wonder!'

After a few meetings, I felt we were making no progress at all on what was supposed to be an important task. Rajeev agreed and said it was best to meet over a lazy dinner so that we both would have enough time and no pressures of work. The dinner was fixed at an Asian food restaurant, which I assumed was a new one and was still to become popular as we were the only two there. I, once again, was carrying several papers and Rajeev had his bag slung diagonally across the body, saying he was prepared.

He insisted we have wine, some nibbles and then move to our agenda. 'Isn't it lovely this evening?' he said clinking my glass, looking at me and then through the large bay windows of the restaurant. He called one of the waiters and whispered in his ear. I was about to say something but he stopped me, 'Wait a minute.'

In less than a minute, the restaurant transformed into a romantic setting. There was a candle on our table and the lights—all of them—had been dimmed! Rajeev smiled, his lips almost pouting while I was stunned, wanting to hide.

This incident resulted in a situation no different from the one I had with Dhirendra, only a few days ago. Rajeev, however, felt I had led him. 'If you weren't interested in me, why were we meeting? Go meet someone you like,' he said in a voice that had inched up a few decibels. 'But you wanted a media plan from me!' I said but Rajeev walked away, waving his hands in disapproval.

What I was left with after these two intriguing encounters was a conclusion that I lacked the finer sense of spotting hints that someone was interested in me.

'It is not just that,' Adi explained, 'there aren't many friends in the gay community, like "regular pals" as heterosexual men put it. So, if someone is breaking away from a "group" and spending time with you—only you—hours or days after the first meeting, it is a sure-shot sign that they are interested in you. So exclusivity and time are indications that you are special and they are looking for a relationship… the rest are just sisters.' He laughed using a term that was popular amongst the community.

There were many types of groups or sub-groups then. Some were for business networking and collaborations using multiple skills to win a project. Others were about hanging out to watch films or head to a party. From there, it was possible for smaller groups to emerge or even just two to become good friends or lovers.

In a sense, Humrahi was the larger group for us and from where other groups emerged. Even Adi, Dheeman had become one such subgroup.

Adi was flamboyant, rarely hiding his sexuality from anyone. He wasn't loud as such but as he said 'his flame was always burning'. He belonged to Lucknow but had been living in Delhi for several years and was a public relations executive with one of the leading firms in the country. He loved food, could talk about almost anything under the sun—except for music. If there was something he feared, it was being found out by his parents or even his sister.

He was shocked to hear about the absence of both love and lust from, what was considered, my long life of thirty! He asked many questions—whether someone in my family had ever violated me, had I ever been with a girl and what was my type?

Apparently, many men had gone through some form of sexual violence usually involving a family member. Such acts of abuse impacted the mental and emotional state of many boys who carried that baggage late into life. I, as fortune had it, had never been through such a ghastly act.

'I had never been with a woman, nor had I any such interest,' I told Adi and Dheeman. 'I was also not bisexual,' I added. However, Adi threw some light on what gay men and their history was like. 'There are men out there who have been with women and have realized later that they are best off with men. That isn't bisexuality as such. It is a choice one makes built on an instinct and comfort,' he explained.

As for a type, I was not sure I had one. I told them of Sufal and Murli and the boy at New Market in Kolkata and then said,

'Well, Dheeman is very attractive.' Adi believed 'attraction' was circumstantial but it seemed I liked slim, small-framed men who had little or no hair on their body. I wasn't sure but he could be right, Dheeman seemed to fit that type just like the others from my past.

We met pretty often during that week and stayed together after the Saturday meeting. I realized that Dheeman and Adi were very close, closer than I was to the two of them. They hung out a lot and had even been to each other's home on a few occasions. One evening, as we celebrated a big 'exclusive' report of mine, something that had landed up as a matter of debate in Parliament, I saw that there was more to their friendship than I knew.

It was on that night, I found their legs touching each other and it seemed intentional rather than by chance. If that was not disturbing, the revelation that he and Dheeman had slept together, knocked my mind and heart over. I, of course, concealed my disappointment.

As they went on their own way, I went on mine, heading back home, upset and angry. I lay on the mattress in Ma's room, crying in an uncontrollable manner. I got out of bed some time during the night and headed to my new room. I threw myself on that single bed, holding a pillow as though it was a human being—a man—I wanted to make love to. My body moved, like I was above someone, indulging in an act of intercourse, consummating nothing at all but my sense of incompleteness.

The tears and the 'lovemaking', with no one but my bed and pillow, did not stop for a while, not until I slept off, exhausted. That night was the first time I slept alone in 'my' room, away from Ma's—a room that all of us had shared at different stages of our lives—for over a decade.

But after that night, I never went back to sleep in Ma's room, making the new room a space for me to grow in.

Chapter Eighteen

'IS EVERYTHING OKAY?' Ma asked the next morning, wondering why I had slept in another room. 'I just felt like sleeping in the new room, Ma. This room was anyway built for me to stay in,' I replied. She smiled. I think Ma thought I was getting over Samrita and the engagement that never happened and might even reconsider meeting prospective girls for marriage. Rita mami—my mother's sister-in-law—had already taken up the burden of finding a suitable match but had been asked to wait till everyone thought I had steadied my ship after the 'jolt' on 11 April.

The April mishap had become a shield. Any suggestion to meet a girl was put off as I needed 'time and space'. Ma as well as Rita mami would say this to friends who had a girl in mind for me; both going by a script that they thought was honest. None of them knew I had already moved on. They neither had any inkling of the delight Humrahi brought me nor the emotional dip I was going through at that point either.

The thought that I stood no chance of being with Dheeman broke my heart. I decided it was best for me to stay away from Adi and Dheeman for a while. I would rather refocus on the Saturday meetings and hope that someone else popped up.

As expected, I would have to meet Rajeev at the meetings. He was cold and made no effort to say hello. I went up to him and apologized and asked if he was well. 'You don't need to know,' he said curtly. I even called him a few days later as it was his birthday.

He took my call and was brief, thanking me. I was not sure if I was doing the right thing by him. Yet I felt it was important to patch up and be friends, if possible, as I may actually have 'led him on'.

What I did not know was Rajeev was not over me. That night, around 2, the phone in our home rang. Given that we had extensions in Ma's room, the living room and my new room in addition to the primary line close to the main door, we had as many as four phones ringing in unison. I woke up with a start and rushed to the phone to find Rajeev whispering loudly that he was sorry he had been curt and did not thank me enough earlier in the day. This incident repeated itself the following night, waking Ma up too. Thankfully, I beat her to the phone.

Rajeev wanted to talk to me or as he said 'he wanted to hear my voice'. I had no option but to be abrupt and tell him that calling at that hour was not okay and he was disturbing not only my sleep but Ma's too. He thought I was being rude. As I put the phone back on its cradle, I knew this conversation had put a lid on any connection left with Rajeev.

Ma was curious about the calls and was aware I had taken them and spoken to someone. I told her that it was a colleague who had moved to Delhi recently and was going through a bad marriage. 'Have I met her?' she asked and I said 'not yet' as she had not been around the last office party I had held at home.

As I covered up, I wondered how long I could keep up this facade and keep lying to her. How many stories was I to spin still? What would happen if Ma got to know the truth, and that too not from me?

I wanted to talk to someone and wished I had Adi with me—the only good listener I knew and a person who had the knack of being supportive and understanding, often providing some interesting insight. For around ten days now, I was not returning calls from him or Dheeman, still not willing to accept them as a couple. But as I look back, I think I was seeking attention, seeing if they missed my presence at all and whether Dheeman was happy without me.

About a week later, it so happened that Adi called not once but maybe a dozen times. Assuming there could be an emergency, I finally took his call. 'Where have you been and why have you not been in touch?' he asked. I claimed to be busy and preoccupied. 'Oh come on, you can't be that busy,' Adi said in disbelief and quickly started gossiping about the gay scene—who was out with whom and so on, giving me no chance to cut the conversation. He had just lightened things up and I was elated getting back with him.

Now it was my turn to update him. I had to offload the anguish caused by Rajeev's late night calls. I explained how I was unused to a parallel life and that I could not keep telling lies. 'One day I might forget what the story was and get caught,' I told the two of them.

They had met Ma briefly when they had dropped by a few days after my birthday that September. I remember Ma looking at them curiously, not knowing who they were. She must have ruled out any connection with *The Economic Times* or journalism as they both looked very young. Dheeman was just nineteen years old. Also, neither of them had the carefree, careless and curious look that reporters had where the sense of self was not defined by what one wore.

According to Adi, Ma was a sensitive and kind person. 'I can't say what may happen if you come out to her. It can be a shock or she may just accept things the way they are. Under any circumstances, I am there,' he reassured me, giving me a tight hug.

I realized that I needed someone from the world I had been familiar with, someone Ma was aware of and who carried enough weight for her to listen to, if required. This is why I turned to Venu and Chitra.

Venu was naturally charming, calm and analytical. He had the ability to apply philosophy to the most mundane of things, making them seem more interesting than they normally were. Chitra was similar in nature and was instinctively helpful, even reading situations remotely. Both of them had the ability to rationalize and then accept things for what they were while making a choice on the battles they picked.

It was the month of October when I decided to take four days off from work. My plan was this—I would come out to Ma on day two after I came out to Venu and Chitra on the first day of my break. The remaining two days were a buffer, for any eventuality, a showdown with Ma or that I would have to pack up and leave home, a possibility that I hoped would never happen.

No matter what the outcome was of 'coming out', I was once again embarking on something new in an already unfamiliar time of life.

Chapter Nineteen

IT WAS 7 October, the first day of my short four-day break from work. That same evening, I was supposed to be at Venu and Chitra's home for dinner. On reaching their home, my nervousness came to the fore delaying any conversation about my sexuality, even though I had already told them there was something urgent and important I wanted to share.

From pre-dinner to dinner to after the meal, clearing up the table, I kept saying 'later'. It was easy to take Venu off track as he was almost obsessed by news and the analysis of stories that flashed on TV and appeared in print. It was a busy year because of the Kargil war, the politics that followed and debates that continued till much after summer on how the media had reported from the region. If I remember correctly, there were discussions about pro-independence groups in Kashmir as well as the expectation of an order from the Supreme Court on four conspirators involved in the assassination of Rajiv Gandhi.

We talked about these developments that were terribly irrelevant to my predicament but important enough to give me some time before I finally came out to them.

Actually, it was Chitra who brought things to focus, as we placed the dishes in the kitchen. I was asked to sit on the single-seater sofa bang opposite her as Venu relaxed on a divan. 'Everything else can wait, first, you tell us what is bugging you,' she said.

I had no option now and this is what I said, 'Every Saturday

I go to a meeting. It is a group called Humrahi. The meeting is hosted by Naz Foundation and—' Chitra cut me short and immediately took over, 'Anjali Gopalan's Naz Foundation? Have you met Saleem?' I said yes to both the questions.

Saleem was one of the senior gay men who came for these meetings occasionally. A noted historian, professor and author, Saleem Kidwai, was a friend of Venu and Chitra and the co-author of *Same-Sex Love in India*, a book that was released the following year. Chitra's connection with him was not about his sexuality but was to do with art and history and that he belonged to a family of Sufi saints.

I had not used the word gay or homosexual so far or even later in the conversation. I didn't have to. Their response to the little I had said so far was so non-discriminatory, taking me as just another guy who had a different sexual orientation. Adding to the calm, Venu revealed he had some inkling about my sexuality, 'Didn't I tell you that Sharif may say this!' He looked at Chitra.

They were both interested in what the meetings were like, if I had been to any parties yet and what was it like in the group of people I had met so far. Everything was so easy; I seemed to be the same person I was for them since the time we had first met.

'So what's the problem? Asked Chitra. I told them that I foresaw issues with Ma and was not sure how she'd respond to knowing about my sexuality. I wanted to come out to her so that I could stop lying and realized that telling her the truth was the only way.

The two of them knew that Ma and I had an equation that not too many parents shared with their children—she enjoyed some of the music I listened to, we watched television over dinner almost every evening, we shopped together, and if Ma was invited to a family get-together, the invitation would be extended to me even if cousins of my generation were not there.

Similarly, when I had colleagues over, Ma would almost be at the centre of the party, sometimes dancing with them, at other times having long conversations. Some of my colleagues had also become her patients. With the kind of proximity we shared, and Ma not being social as such, my network had kind of become hers too.

Chitra and Venu, of course, saw this context as a positive. 'This is why we don't think you have a reason to fear,' said Chitra. They were certain Ma was a strong person by nature and could weather any storm. Just like I was feeling a growing distance as my lies to her mounted over the past two months or so, Ma also would not wish for anything that would take us apart, the two of them explained, making sense of the confusion I found myself in.

The conversation lightened up as Venu was still basking in his successful bulls eye reading of my sexuality. It seems my interest in Saran's *Summer in My Veins*—something I spoke about in the bureau once—had not gone unnoticed as I hardly ever spoke of films at work. Also, the way I described women was never the way men in general did, there was no show of machoism or the overpowering sense of lust. My observations, as per him, were more to do with their jewellery, their eyes and smile, and what they wore instead of their physical attributes like breasts, lips, waist and hips.

Chapter Twenty

THAT NIGHT, THE reassurance from Venu and Chitra gave me a great sense of determination to move forward in life, not thinking of hindrances.

By the next morning, however, all of this diminished, leaving me with cold feet and a desire to postpone my intended conversation with Ma. The whole of Friday went by aimlessly and Saturday was no better. Adi, who was still to come out to his parents but was in no hurry to do so as he was living independently and alone in Delhi, called to check on my 'coming out' experience and was disappointed to hear where things stood. 'Postponing this will not change things, you are not in my situation. You live with Aunty and are too close to allow a distance,' he said plainly. I agreed but was still apprehensive.

I was down to the last day—Sunday—of my very short break. I opened my room door and walked towards the telephone table next to the main door to pick up the *Sunday Economic Times* from the pile of newspapers. As I turned around, now facing the kitchen that was in front of the main door, I saw Ma and wished her good morning.

She was in the kitchen, standing in front of the stove. Both her hands were busy, holding coloured supplements. Ma walked up towards me, moving away from the gas stove on which some tea was brewing. 'Have you seen this?' she asked, referring to the papers in her hands. They were partially folded; I could not read a thing. The special features, from two different publications, were on marriage bureaus, I realized.

'Oh no, I don't want to read this,' I said turning away and moving out of the kitchen in disgust.

She followed me out and urged me to give her a listen. A friend of mine from the colony, Gopal, had told Ma that marriage bureaus were helpful organizations and will supplement the efforts of Rita mami in finding a girl for me. All I had to do, Ma explained, was to submit my biodata and other required details and the bureau would take care of the rest, which would be to line up girl after girl, I guess.

That moment was as unanticipated as it could ever be—there I was with an incomplete agenda after wasting three days and there she was standing innocently with no knowledge of who I was. While I sighed and wished to raise my voice, I gently asked her to come to my room, 'I need to talk to you, Ma.'

Ma returned to the kitchen, made some tea and brought it to my room. We sat on the slim single bed I had. The supplements were still with her. I took them, placed them on the side of the bed and started to talk.

I looked down at the floor, not sure if I could look straight in her face, and told her I didn't wish to marry and I was never going to. I paused, looked up, expecting Ma to respond but she was silent, only her expression had changed. She looked confused. There must have been many questions tossing in her mind, waiting to be asked. 'I am not interested in women. I am not attracted to any,' I explained. 'I am gay, Ma.'

'Gay?' she asked, looking absolutely puzzled. The word 'gay' obviously meant nothing to her as she had never heard it being used in relation to marriage or a person as such. It always meant happy, in any other form of usage, after all.

'I am homosexual. I am attracted to men, this is what the word gay means,' I replied, simplifying matters in the only way I knew at that point. 'Do you think women are ugly? That is why you are not attracted to them? I don't understand,' she reacted.

I struggled at that moment, saying just one thing, over and over again, 'I like men and I am attracted to them.' I was sounding more certain. I think I was a little irritated too, not by her questions, but my inability to find better words and explanations. 'Men don't get married to other men,' I added thinking that I had hit the nail on the head.

I don't know what went through Ma's mind but she did not seem puzzled or even fazed. She looked calm or maybe that was just a pretence. 'Ma, there are many beautiful women. Madhuri Dixit, for example, is gorgeous. Her smile, the way she uses her eyes is all beautiful. But, I am not attracted to her or any of these beautiful aspects of a woman,' I continued, not sure I should have.

Ma had not finished. The questions that followed though were exemplary, keeping in mind the year and time in which they were asked. The first question was, 'Is there someone in your life?' Question two was about Adi and Dheeman and whether they were homosexuals. Question three was whether they were a couple? The answers were no, yes and yes, respectively.

Ma wasn't done though. She was curious to know where I had met them and whether I was meeting other men. I told her about the Humrahi group and the structured meetings organized by Anjali's Naz Foundation. This is when I admitted I had been lying about the workshops on intellectual property.

She then named friend after friend asking me if I found any of them attractive. It was only when she named Asif—a young Middle Eastern boy in his early 20s who worked in our office in the administration section—that I stopped her and said I found him very handsome. Ma had met him several times as he and I had become friends. He had also come to some of the get-togethers held at home.

'He is a very nice boy, soft-spoken and seems to come from

a good family,' Ma observed. She asked if I had told him what I felt. Of course, I hadn't and I told her so.

Ma got up, picked up the newspapers, the cups of tea, suggesting I get ready for our Sunday outing. It was like nothing had happened or changed. I was amazed and thrilled waiting to share this with Venu, Chitra and Adi. Chitra and Venu were happy for me, adding that I should never underestimate my mother. Adi, of course, was also thrilled and now was keen to come home and spend some time with Ma and me.

We were soon out of the house, heading towards Central Market in Lajpat Nagar. This is where we picked up our supply of salted snacks and dry fruits. Ma occasionally bought cloth by the metre from some of the stores. But on that day, we walked in to a popular clothes store that kept shirts and pants confiscated by the customs department. Ma bought me a checked shirt—a Tom Tailor—that I still have hanging in my cupboard. My eyes were moist as I looked away, holding the bag with the shirt in it, feeling I had been rewarded for telling her the truth and more so for how she had received it.

As we drove back home, Ma posed a few more questions, obviously her mind was at work. Was Samrita aware of my sexuality? Is this why the engagement was called off? Did I tell her? I was taken aback but calmly said no, she wasn't aware. I felt Ma had just heaved a sigh of relief and that left me very relaxed too!

Chapter Twenty-one

SOON AFTER THAT eventful and smooth Sunday, I connected with my brothers—Dilip living in West Hartford, US, and Duji in London—through a conference call. I wasted no time and told them that I was gay and had come out to Ma too the day before.

The call was a cakewalk and I think I sounded like a kid with a new toy to talk about. I had felt sure that my brothers would support me but what I didn't expect was Duji sounding celebratory and Dilip expressing caution. What was a revelation though was that my sexuality had been discussed at different junctures between my bothers and their wives, who I spoke to one by one, soon after.

'About time!' said Peggy who had been dead sure I was gay and had suspected so since 1993, when we had first met. One morning, as per her account, I walked out of the toilet after taking a shower wearing nothing but a towel wrapped around my waist. 'You never once felt uncomfortable, you continued to dress yourself, as though I didn't exist even though we kept talking,' she said. 'This is not what heterosexual men do and you know what, I didn't feel threatened,' she added, putting into perspective the normal equations that heterosexual men and women had.

'You did not seem like the classic alpha male. You were fastidious about what you wore, not a fashionista but surely selective and neat.' Apparently, when I had introduced her to Samrita, I had appeared 'weirdly formal and out of sorts', more indications that I was undeniably not heterosexual.

Sonu, however, had a slightly different take. 'At first, I thought perhaps your awkwardness came from being overweight, but later even after you lost some weight, you sort of never seemed at ease.' What they all discussed was my closeness to Ma. 'You were way closer to her than you were to your brothers which seemed odd because we were all in our 20s,' she said. While they all gelled as a group and hung out and shared stuff, I somehow never became a part of that group, remaining aloof, Sonu had observed.

Even Sonu's brother-in-law, Allen, who had come to meet her, never thought I was 'straight'. As the story goes, I walked up to them wearing a white banyan, an oversized pair of black shorts with a pair of long white soccer socks pulled up to my knees. 'You said a quick hello, looked very uncomfortable and left immediately. And as soon as you stepped out of the room Allen commented, "I didn't know Dilip's brother was gay".'

When I asked why none of them ever broached the subject of my sexuality, Duji said, 'We were never dead sure and it could be offensive and alienating. Also, we've known of gay men who ran away from home when confronted with the truth by someone else.'

It is not always the initial question but the scary prospects of what follows after saying yes, I realized which in many cases is anger and abuse, or even being thrown out of a home. And such questions, particularly at a time when one is not ready to probably even say yes to oneself at first, is scarier. Hence, clearly picking a moment to speak up or to say yes, was always ours, I learnt.

I am not sure what it would have been like had they made subtle hints, asking me about dates with women, my taste in girls—conversations they were used to. Would that have changed the course of my life, I wonder. Or would that have made me paranoid?

Either way, at that moment, hearing all of this, I knew there was strong support from across my family. It was hard for me though to assimilate all the indicators of my sexuality identified by them. I mean, I never liked hair on my legs but was wearing socks the way I had an indication of my queerness? Or that I did not hang out with them or my closeness to Ma?

If anything made sense, it was the accepted pattern that most gay men were very close to their mothers. And if their mothers were widowed or divorced, there was a tendency amongst both of them to let their lives revolve around each other, even unintentionally denying space to explore their lives independently, providing mutual pillars of support. This proximity, I learnt, had a lot to do with the hostility and alienation that was often prevalent outside the home for both—a widow and gay man—in different measure.

Even as I lapped up all the support and affection over the phone calls, Dilip's words of caution did linger in my mind for a while. 'Not everyone will accept your sexuality and things could be hard at your workplace.' Even when I told him that I had Venu as my boss, Dilip felt that 'it was not about one person or two, it was the ecosystem'.

While he partially raised the red flag, his concerns weren't misplaced and years later were even backed by research. A human rights campaign recently said over 51 per cent of LGBTQ workers hide their identity in 'liberal' US. Another research article from the same country said that over 65 per cent of LGBT persons felt workplace culture had impacted them psychologically. 'Just imagine how horrid it could be in India,' my eldest brother commented, suggesting relocating out of Delhi and India, rekindling work offers I had at one time. I, of course, never did that. I was blessed having the family I had, Ma in particular.

As I grew into the community, I became more aware of how difficult life was for even people known to me and close to our group. I lost three acquaintances to suicides. A man who used to hang out in our group and had a gay-friendly boss went on to get married as his family was known to sacrifice anyone in the name of honour. Another friend from a very elite family was not allowed to have his boyfriend sit at the same dinner table if the parents were present. And then there were some who lost their jobs for their 'queerness' even if it was just painting their nails and appearing 'effeminate'!

Clearly, even privilege and access to a system in mainstream and modern Delhi did not necessarily mean there would be acceptance and support. The faultlines, as it was, were there to be seen.

Chapter Twenty-two

THE PARALLEL LIFE I was leading blurred almost immediately, making it easier for me to step out and meet people knowing that none of this was a secret from Ma. Adi came over more often, so did Dheeman, sometimes together. Adi, given his outgoing nature, got closer to Ma—they had a strong connection that exists even today, and is stronger than before. He would charm her with his skills in the kitchen and with flowers he brought for her on many occasions.

I also started hosting small dinners at home with my new gay group. For Ma's comfort, and I think for mine too, I had Chitra and Venu as part of these occasions particularly if Saleem was amongst the guests. They were like a bridge, in a manner of speaking, bringing my two worlds together.

According to Venu, while Ma spoke to everyone, she looked a tad bit uncertain of how to conduct herself with this new group. I believed that she was carrying the same apprehensions I had when I first attended the Humrahi meeting. Yet, he was also sure that Ma was observing every action, conversation and behaviour to find something distinct or just to learn and adapt to the community. 'She is very sharp, extremely wise, so don't be surprised if she asks questions.' Venu unknowingly peeped into the future.

On one occasion, Ma produced a news report that appeared in a popular English daily claiming that homoeopathy had a 'cure' for homosexuality, directly defining sexual orientation as a disease.

'Have you seen this?' she asked. I was surprised and angered. 'Are you saying I am sick, Ma? What I am and who I am is natural, it is not an ailment that any medicine can cure.' My voice was louder than normal. I recall Ma looking a bit scared, unsure of how to respond. 'I am just sharing the news report,' she said quickly dumping it in the dustbin.

This led to other questions a few days later: what attracted me to men and what happens when I see someone I like? While she was seeking information, I somehow felt there was an element of doubt in her mind on the definitiveness of me being gay. I started by telling Ma that I found them beautiful and they attracted me. I added that it could be their face, the collarbones, the slimness or even the 'waif look' that often caught my eye. I remember mentioning Jakob Dylan—the son of my intellectual guru, Bob Dylan—who I felt was a hottie. That answer was not enough for her.

'What happens? I mean what do you go through?' She persisted. Frustrated and annoyed, I put things plainly saying the uncensored, 'I get a hard-on!' This reply put an end to the conversation and for a very long time, Ma never posed a single question to me that had sexuality as a part of it.

I, however, wondered how had she remained so calm initially when I had come out. I also wondered why she produced the newspaper article—was she still in doubt or hoping I would be 'straight', like other parents who insisted their children were unaware of their sexuality and required medical help.

When I asked her, months later, she said softly, 'I did not understand everything you said but when you told me you were gay, I felt sad that you had to keep a secret with yourself for so long. This is what came to me first.' She paused and added, 'From there on, it was a learning process and I did not know what to believe as whatever information was available concluded that you were suffering from a disease and did not know how to deal with it. Society in any case can be unforgiving when it is anything odd and definitely if it is a mental health issue. I just wanted to protect you.'

Ma apparently started reading newspapers, front to back, to spot any news story or feature that used the words 'gay' or 'homosexual'. It was her way of learning to know me better, even if a report misled her into believing an untruth. She even discussed my life with my brothers, initially disagreeing with them, going by reports stating there was a cure. It was not necessarily denial as much as her instinct to care and the fear of how society reacts.

She, like any other mother, believed I should be safe and careful, given the general connection between homosexuality and AIDS. She would regularly ask if I was sufficiently aware about HIV and whether I had been tested. As we relaxed a lot more on the subject of my sexuality, she would cutely ask whether I was dating someone or if there was someone special.

I did once tell her that I fancied Dheeman but would never wish to put my friendship with Adi at risk. 'Have you considered speaking with Asif, your colleague?' she asked. I hadn't till then, but planned to do so soon.

As per assumptions of the group I hung out with, Middle Eastern men were not just good-looking but were known to be bisexual. There was also a belief that there was a large homosexual population living there underground, just like in India. While none of this could be verified, I took the step forward.

Asif was a slim fair boy, who had a broken milk tooth that made his smile unique and which I found beautiful. It was difficult to believe he could get angry. If he had ever been so, it was so controlled that I didn't even know his temper had ever risen.

I would pick him up early morning from his home in East of Kailash and we would head to office together. Although I was not expected to reach the bureau until after 11 a.m. or closer to lunch, I was in by 9.30 a.m. I usually left when he wound up his work. However, there were times when he would wait for me.

Occasionally, he came home for dinner or lunch and I would go over to have the delicious meals his mother cooked. She was a great cook, churning out a biryani, exposing me to their kind of bread, bringing me closer and closer to who they were.

I never realized that I would ever get jealous but I did on several occasions when Asif got delayed having a conversation with a good-looking guy from another department or newspaper. I tended to keep quiet on our drive back during those instances, and he would always notice my silence, asking if all was well. I would say yes or not reply at all.

I remember finding a notepad full of descriptions of my interactions with Asif, written before I had come out to my family. I had never written such notes for anyone else. While Asif treated me as a dear friend or an elder brother, I had grown fond enough to fall in love with him, had he been gay.

So finally, after a lot of contemplation, I told Asif I was gay. He smiled, his usual loving smile. His head, if I remember correctly, tilted a bit to one side as he said, 'Are you sure? Does your mother know? Wow! This is a surprise!' As the truth trickled into his mind, he asked me if I was seeing someone. Later, he held my hand with both of his and said, 'I don't know what it is like but I hope you find a person who cares for you.'

Our sexuality did not come in the way of our friendship. I was disappointed that he was straight but I had one more person to share my experiences with, however little or insignificant they were. I remember him asking whether others at office knew of me. I told him that Venu did. 'I think it is time you told Rumy and Shalini,' he advised.

Shalini was a strong, dominating lady who was extremely fond of me and was very protective. She was like the mother hen in our bureau but less intrusive than such people were normally known to be. She treated me like I were her younger brother.

Rumy, on the other hand, was a young, independent sort of

girl who had moved to Delhi about a year back from Mumbai. She was struggling with the culture of the city and its people, but she found me different from the usual 'Delhi types'.

I took Shalini out for lunch and midway through the meal, I told her I was gay and she need not look for a girl for me. Shalini seemed surprised, her eyes got larger, the eyebrows moved up and she stopped sipping her soft drink. From being a warm-hearted person, always looking out for me, she suddenly turned a bit cold, almost dismissing everything I told her. She was disinterested, not asking me any questions about my experiences.

While this was a let-down, I had more surprises coming my way. A rumour went around that I had tried to come on to another colleague who was the fittest in the team and arguably the most attractive. He always had women swooning over him and now, as per the rumours, he had a man desiring him as well. This was a double whammy; not only was my sexuality put out there but these alleged 'advances' were called perverse, defining my character.

Months later, after I had quit *The Economic Times* and had moved with Venu to a dot-com, my Hotmail account was hacked by someone, probably a former colleague. An email between my brothers and I reached the inbox of more than one person. The email had details on an evening that Adi, Dheeman and I had spent at an ice-cream parlour, ogling at men. I got to know this when a senior editor and a former colleague at the newspaper shared that email with me, stating, 'I don't think this was for me'.

I felt violated, flustered, anxious and angered. I was unsure of what I should do, other than change my password. I didn't know who was to blame and why someone would do this.

Yet, if there was an upper, it was Rumy who responded with excitement about my sexuality although turning me into a product. 'You are marketable, brands look for people like you,' she said joyously and with absolute innocence and dedication to her work in brand equity (where everything was about products). She was right though as there was a commercial world out there that referred to gay couples as DINK—double income no kids. Of course, this was long before same-sex marriage became legal and adoption was allowed.

Even though, in her naivety, she had turned me into a product of economic relevance, Rumy's love and care for me went a lot beyond that. The girl who wanted to go out on weekends to parties with me was now a supportive person who was always willing to be 'my girl' at events and get-togethers that were for 'couples' only—as per the rules laid down by just about any hospitality (ironically) unit that ran bars, discos and nightclubs. Of course, society at that point equated us—gay couples—with stags that posed a threat to women, obviously unaware how threatened we were.

Rumy and I had regular arguments on choice, liberation and which men we fancied. But when I talked about the waif look and said I found Jakob Dylan hot, she, miraculously, agreed with me! We would jabber over coffee, head to markets and even pick a corner at office to catch up, sometimes on nothing.

'I am your fag hag,' she said triumphantly. 'Fag hag' was a term that was relatively new to me. It was a slang term that defined women who hung out or were associated closely with gay and bisexual men. The word fag and fag hag (as a term) were initially considered offensive as they were invariably used in a derogatory manner.

With time, the terms got absorbed into 'our' vocabulary, being used in a positive manner. Even the word queer, which once had a negative connotation, is now an umbrella word for the community. We claim queer means 'extraordinary'.

On a couple of occasions Rumy had commented that hanging out with me was not only about fun, shopping for clothes and talking about men, but she felt safe. Even Sudha echoed this. 'When I am out with a gay man, I am least bothered whether my cleavage shows, or my arms are flabby or if my hips are too large.' In any state or form, a gay man did not judge or scrutinize a woman the way many lecherous men did, she said.

There were other reasons why gay men and heterosexual women got along and made good friends. The sense of adversity, and the challenges emanating from patriarchy were common to both. And the fact that we both sought men was another factor that brought us together.

Specifically for me at this stage of life and learning, every person who accepted me was an addition to my support system. It was one more person I could share my life with and not feel odd or awkward around. Rumy was one of them and fortunately Shalini was slowly returning to who she had always been—a caring person, calling me over for dinner several times.

Chapter Twenty-three

I HAD ALSO started to observe myself, spending time almost every night before sleeping, introspecting and reflecting on who I was and how I was not the person I used to be. My greatest influence, of course, was the community itself which was dynamic, constantly learning off each other, living off whatever was possible, creating one's own world.

Undoubtedly, we lived in the dark shadows of big cities, meeting strangers, creating our groups, striving hard to find spaces, living boldly while knowing how much we feared being found out or caught. There were horror stories of rape not just by family members but also by law enforcers who picked up men in parks that were used as 'cruising' spots. I remember being told how some had experienced the ghastly act of a stick being shoved up their rear by an angry father or even a policeman. In some cases, the offender would violently indulge in unsafe sex, adding to the trauma of sexual violence.

Even with this backdrop, something I had been protected from—the community laughed, danced, made love repeatedly.

As was expected, we talked about men, the ones we saw in movies or models in advertisements. It wasn't unusual to hope that every model or actor was actually gay or bisexual. 'None of them had tried to sleep with a man,' as one of my friends used to say.

I remember how many suggested, clinging to the thinnest of threads, that the world was changing, that the 'complete man' in the Raymond's ad had gay 'characteristics'. We had all seen a slight shift in the depiction of a male person. It was moving away from the alpha male who was never seen to 'feel' or be 'sensitive' towards the 'complete man' who was caring for a pet, emoting with a father or mother (in particular), and showing a softer side that we generally attribute to ourselves.

There was also an assumption that the 'metrosexual man' was again a depiction of who we were as people, even though the term was coined to describe a single heterosexual man living in an urban environment. However, the common ground was the prevalence of singlehood, the meticulous grooming and the time spent shopping for oneself. Even as we drew parallels, our hope did turn out to be true with many blogs several years later claiming exactly this or at least saying metrosexual applied to gay and bisexual men, with one rider—you must have disposable income!

The closest I came to a 'gay connection' in the mainstream world was Freddie Mercury of the band Queen and Boy George of Culture Club. While I loved their songs like 'I Want to Break Free' by Queen and 'Karma Chameleon' of Culture Club, I started to give them a special place in my collection of music, something I hadn't done till then.

I was clearly a slow and late starter, older than most in that group barring probably Saleem and a couple of others, struggling to keep pace with their idea of life. Even my sex life was an embarrassment because in that group my inexperience was considered a failing and not purity as celebrated in society. 'How could you survive in that world for so long?' I was asked with admiration, disdain and kilos of disbelief whenever someone found out I was still a virgin. The kiss and body-to-body intimacy with Sufal did not count. 'Have you considered priesthood, or turning into a monk or a pujari?' I was asked jokingly with a comment being provided immediately, 'Yes, no or *nun* of the above!'

While I felt awkward I knew it was all in fun and that perhaps many were waiting to 'do' me—as Adi had once said—there is something special about 'deflowering' someone.

Conversations, as they were, had an element of carelessness and lots of sexual overtones to be precise. If the length of the organ, the penis that is, was not under discussion, it was the girth. If it was neither of the two, it was about penetration, the crack between the cheeks and how deep one had been.

Then, there was something called rimming, or to rim which was basically the tongue between the cheeks and not in the way that one assumes as sarcasm or a manner of speaking. The cheeks, just to clarify, were the two sides of the butt, the tongue would kind of line the crack, relaxing the muscles in that area. Imagine how much we laughed when a telecom company launched RIM!

The smartness of the chatter was such that I could not merely assume things and depend on the Oxford English Dictionary or Webster's Dictionary or even Roget's Thesaurus to find my way through a conversation. I realized 'our' language had its own nuances and usage.

Jerks, for example, were not merely people. It could be the act of masturbation or the simple action of pushing or actually being pushed while in bed with someone or being penetrated by a chugging steam train that jerked its way forward.

Also, you rarely 'took a position' on anything except when you were with your sex partner! So, if you were in the midst of a serious discussion on human rights and were asked to 'take a position', it wasn't surprising if someone said 69.

Even if you rushed down the stairs, as many of us did after the Humrahi meeting, it was risky to say you 'were going down' because that was just another sexual act and 'on whom?' was the often-heard response. And, you could never come (cum) from behind because how could you!

Even an innocent courtesy 'how do you do?' could lead to an unexpected 'come home and I can show you how' response. And just imagine what a 'head-on collision' could mean or the 'Big Bang' or even 'organic growth', and whether you made a 'sizeable difference' or not.

No wonder there were some creatively titled pornographic films such as 'Schindler's Fist', 'Cum, Watt, May' and 'Get Down Tonight', to name just a few, catering to the peculiar yet brilliant gay sense of humour.

I learnt other things that were more important than wit. There were tops, bottoms, kings and queens. These words determined your role in sex. A queen and bottom were the same—the one who got penetrated or the woman in the sexual act. The top or king was the dominant partner, penetrating the bottom. And then there was the versatile—one who could be both, the top and the bottom.

On paper and in conversations, all of this may seem as loose talk and slutty but in reality, this was far more important than wit and humour. I realized that a king and king would most likely not make a couple. The same would be for a bottom and a bottom. There were exceptions, of course, where a third party–a bottom for two tops or a top for two bottoms—was invited to fulfil the desire for sex.

This was a huge learning for me as I wondered what role I would play if I were to fall in love. At that point, my only idea of sex was to do with love and a body-to-body interaction. I remember a few other men at that time seemed very similar in their thought process, not knowing what role they may take when in bed.

I guess we all had to think this through at some point. I did and remember feeling that I wished to dominate in bed but was also open to being submissive. I wasn't a hundred per cent sure what role I might play when I eventually have sex! I was, however, dead sure that finding the right man and love was of greater importance.

Chapter Twenty-four

AMONGST THE MANY ways to find a man, was to head out to gay parties. Those were the days of party organizers that had the exceptional ability to build diaries of phone numbers of people like us mostly through word of mouth. Interestingly, lots of the numbers had no names—unless someone volunteered to reveal their identity. The question of privacy generally never arose as the hosts were trusted enough not to share names or numbers.

Yet, there were many people I knew who had two numbers—one for the gay world (including the party circuit) and the other for the rest. And yes, nicknames, as it were, was another veil of protection.

Another unique characteristic of that time was that no list focused on income or status or the language a person spoke. As a result, parties had a great mix of people, reflecting a social mobility that Delhi was not known for. Entry fees did sift people out though. Still, given the desperate need to have one's own space to release the tension and stress of being confined to the trappings of society, lots of us saved up for that one night out, a seductive liberation that was most definitely a need.

We were so desperate for 'happy' spaces we rarely noticed or just ignored the flaws and discrimination that occurred within the community. Cross-dressers and trans-genders had no place at such parties. In fact, some invitations clearly stated the entry bar. I wasn't aware of anyone who raised a voice against such rules and if someone had, it did not seem to bring a visible change at the parties that I had been to. Even I was guilty of remaining silent, selfishly enjoying the 'treasured' night outs we had.

What I also got to know was that there were farmhouse parties, mostly tucked away in the then dingy Mehrauli area, and private parties at homes. And there was the occasional glimmer of hope when a bar opened its doors to us.

While many of the organizers were from the community, some did belong to the heterosexual world who had realized that we were an economic opportunity and hence had swooped in to leverage our plight and income to their benefit. It wasn't unusual, as it is today as well, for many 'heterosexual' men to offer themselves at a price for a quickie or a long night of sex with sleepover, luring some into wanting more. These were perilous interactions for sure, but they were definitely less risky than being outted!

Farmhouse parties, in particular, were seedy in nature and that itself was their charm what with the expanse of space, the psychedelic dance floors, the DJs who were open to taking requests, the dark bushes and the odd game revolving around language and sexual innuendoes. At that time, the entry charges ranged from ₹250 to ₹500, offering a hard drink or food or both.

Private parties, however, were more controlled with mostly friends and friends of friends organizing and contributing to it with snacks or alcohol and bottles of Coke and soda. Such get-togethers were perhaps the only time lesbians were seen. This is what I noticed in the first such get-together I had been to at the beginning of year 2000.

But, before that, my first-ever party was around four months after coming out—18 December 1999, to be precise. There was a discussion during the Humrahi meeting about the party. It was only after some deliberation and a lot of convincing by Adi that I took the plunge, tying up with him and Dheeman, offering to drive them there and back.

The party was in a multi-storey building in Noida. The first few floors were usually used for weddings and other events; the mezzanine had a billiards table and table tennis facilities that we had access to. The party, though, with the bar and the dancing area, was up on the terrace.

What I saw was a depiction of a gay underbelly that the National Capital Region was unaware of. So was I, till that moment. It was all so unfamiliar and yet attractive, with a positive energy of freedom.

There were eyes reaching out to eyes, kisses flying across the dance floor, bodies touching each other deliberately and sometimes by chance, and exaggerated movements that I had never seen before. There were tongues swaying deep into mouths, legs between legs and the occasional near-making-out scene that many stood on the side watching, criticizing, judging or applauding.

It seemed—from some conversations I had that night with men wearing glitter, high heels, overlayered make-up, great styles and form—that they were all aware that there were no guarantees and no structures, and, therefore, no certainty of who you would be with. So, as one said, 'What's the harm in trying, even if the relationship lasts a year or a few days or a few hours, at least the search for love and pleasures that goes with it would stop for that while.' True as this was, it was a reality I was not comfortable with.

As I scanned the terrace, someone standing close to me said, 'Do remember to get a drink, as it helps to "liquidate" your "assets" and get good "value".' It took me a few minutes to realize I was being hit on. I politely moved away.

I was a hopeless person in search of love, a romantic of sorts, unsure that this is where I would find love. I was literally pulled on to the dance floor by Adi and I found myself dancing with men for the very first time. It took a while to bring some naturalness to my movements but I was finally flowing like the others, although keeping a reasonable distance between the men around me.

The music was great, a pinch of Hindi pop and Bollywood

combined with popular English hits. One of the biggest hits then was Touch & Go's 'Would You…?' which had this pick-up line—would you go to bed with me. This song was repeated a few times and at least twice a young businessman, who was a part of an old alternative medicine company, mouthed this popular pick-up line from the song, directly looking at me, expressing his interest. I would smile and dance on, ignoring his advances but enjoying the unexpected attention.

After a while, I was heading to the toilet on the mezzanine floor. As I walked down, I spotted a fair, broad-shouldered man, with short brown hair, wearing a sky-blue shirt and blue jeans. I had seen him before, not at a gay group meeting but at the repair shop behind Khan Market. He was one of the mechanics who I used to follow with my eyes almost every time I took my car for maintenance check-ups.

I think he spotted me too at that moment as he bent over the billiards table to knock one of the pool balls with the cue. I ran back up and informed Adi of his presence. I wondered if he was gay. Adi, helpful as ever, decided to go and see him and see if his 'gay-dar'—the ability of gay men to spot other gay men—went off. 'You never know,' Adi said returning after screening him from the stairs. 'The mechanic would be aware that it is a gay party and might even know the party organizer, else how could he be here,' Adi said trying to put things into perspective.

I walked to one of the corners of the terrace yet again wondering if I should speak to the mechanic or at least smile and acknowledge his presence. I enjoyed going to the repair shops as there was something delectable about lean, slim and often greased bodies at work. Many of them had large bright eyes, and were often seen smiling, not expressing the pain of their hardships or even when some car owners had been crass and rude. But that man at the party was one who stood out. He usually wore a white T-shirt and faded blue jeans and he never walked around like the others he seemed to strut and even move like a model on a ramp.

My thoughts were interrupted with Adi and Dheeman suggesting we get a round of drinks before leaving for our homes. It was a crowded bar with just two bartenders and maybe at least ten demanding gay men wanting a drink.

As I looked up at the elevated bar, I spotted a young man, a third person next to the bartenders. I think he was just around 5ft 1 inch or 5ft 2 inches. He was fair, slim and had a big smile. I had been told that he was one of the organizers of the party, but no one could confirm his sexuality. He spoke in Hindi and used a few words in English every now and then. He seemed to be very much in charge, ordering the barmen and joining them in preparing the drinks. There was a tinge of anger or arrogance when he spoke to his team but that would change in a split second, when speaking to any of us. I could not put my finger on it but his presence had just made the mechanic irrelevant.

Even as I went home without anyone, feeling alone, the party was extremely relevant, exposing me to another dimension of our community. What I did not know then was that at least one of the men I had set my eyes on that day was going to be a future boyfriend of mine.

Chapter Twenty-five

AS WINTER PEAKED early in January 2000, the number of private parties seemed to increase. I felt a bit more integrated into the community but was still hesitant to take charge of a conversation or approach anyone. However, the fact that I was now being called to private parties was progress of sorts.

It was at one such party held at a home in Green Park that I danced for over an hour and that too with just one person—a dark chocolate-toned boy, fit enough to claim there was no fat on him, short hair and a huge smile that displayed his large buck-teeth. He loved music, so he claimed, and dancing too. It reduced stress, he said. His name was Promit and he was quite popular in the community. I think I had seen him at the Noida party with someone.

After we stopped dancing, I lost sight of him even though the space was not that big. Apparently, people made their moves for each other very quickly, wasting no time so probably Promit was already with another guy, making the party a base to 'shop' in, the term often used by us to find a guy.

It wasn't unusual for someone to use the toilet for a quick make-out session. They could satiate themselves in a few minutes, not knowing when they would get any such space again. I guess I was a turtle then, hardly crawling forward as the world and time passed me by.

Yet, there was something special about this party. I was busy helping the host, Bob, serving honey cookies that I had baked specially for the party and mixing drinks with the Old Monk I had got along. I also stepped into the kitchen, assisting with some meat that was being tossed up in a frying pan. While Bob introduced me to a few of the guests, the honey cookies made me popular for those few hours.

Some of the guys hit on me and said, 'Honey, let the cookie crumble, I am okay with crumbs!' I liked the smart usage of the language but was always slow in responding while continuing to search.

I was soon heading to party after party, ensuring that I had the comfort of Adi with me. I can remember vividly another near disaster as a young fashion designer from Assam came up and danced with me. I must have downed a few drinks to have danced continuously for three or four songs with him, not knowing that he would soon place his hand on my lower back and tug me closer. I was saved by someone who knew him, who started dancing with us, letting me slip off and walk away to Adi, who burst out laughing.

It was then that I spotted someone I had seen earlier at the rooftop party in Noida. It was the bartender. I watched him move around, and then stand at a distance from the crowd. He had a few friends with him and was looking as beautiful as he had the first time I saw him. That night, he wore a beige shirt with black trousers, a few bands on his wrist, the same gentle smile and a mild arrogance that seemed to define a mixed temperament. One of Adi's friends, Karan noticed my gaze fixed at that small group of men. 'Someone interesting?' he asked and I told him who it was.

Unhesitatingly, he walked towards the group of men, pulling me with him, but I lost my nerve and stopped halfway. He went ahead, initiated a conversation, pointed at me, and jotted down something on a piece of paper. That 'something' was his mobile number. As Karan walked back, the boy who's name was Samit, looked at me and smiled.

Samit lived in Delhi's Paharganj area, very close to Connaught Place. His real name, the name he used for a travel agency he ran from his old home, was Deepak. His house looked a lot like a haveli but was far smaller than the ones we see in films. He lived with his mother, was the only child and had given up education after completing school.

While possessing his mobile number was a milestone in itself, it took me a bit of time to connect with him given my typical inhibitions of starting a conversation and to say I was attracted to him. Of course, I finally did so but Samit was not easy to catch hold of. It took weeks to pin him down and to even manage a cup of tea with him.

Although I had said nothing specific on whether I found him attractive or would wish to sleep with him or build a relationship, he knew exactly what I had in mind because he smiled and placed his hand over my thigh, rubbing it as I drove him back to Paharganj after our cup of tea. '*Ek din milte hain* (We will meet one day),' he said with a twinkle in his eyes.

He and I decided we should spend a weekend together sometime soon. On Adi's advice, it was best to pick a guest house rather than take him home. I couldn't agree more as I was not sure how Ma would respond to me having a stranger over, someone I had not even spent more than an hour with. Besides, I was told, the rule was to exercise caution particularly if a 'pick-up', so to speak, was not from a common or familiar group of the community. The fear was that he may not be gay and might be a blackmailer—an extreme thought, I felt, believing Samit was not such a person.

Yet, there were stories of blackmailing and thefts. Even now such crimes lurk on gay chat sites. But as a community, we were used to meeting strangers, some of whom became friends, lovers and partners and others were forgettable experiences not because of bad sex or a terrible relationship but due to crimes that could not be reported to the police. The circumstances of blackmailing or robbery or violence, would not just out the victim but also victimize him in the eyes of society that hated us, and the reference to anything we called sex. Even the police was hardly an ally as it used Section 377 against us and was known to blackmail people like us, making a quick buck whenever possible or forcing their organ into someone's backside for their own pleasure, never once considering it rape or sexual abuse.

Still, these were risks many took given the few and slim options they had. It was in stark contrast with the heterosexual world that had the luxury of meeting potential lovers and partners through friends, family, workplaces, hobby and recreational groups besides classified advertisements, all of which created their own filters. Those filters and structures created 'safe' grounds and spaces that let them evolve, flower and find others—so many who didn't have to ever think of being 'outed' or 'coming out'.

If there was anything distantly similar, a filter creating safety of sorts, it was the Humrahi group—where members were largely culturally and economically in the same bracket. There were other groups that emerged through NGOs too, where again economics, culture and language brought people together with their sexuality being the other commonality.

But I, like many others, was a hopeless romantic believing love would conquer anything. And for some reason—blinding love as Adi put it—did not allow me to think Samit was a risk at all.

During that time, Adi and I had some of the most exciting evenings after work. We hopped around from one guest house to another, checking out rooms and the price thereof. We visited places in Kailash Colony, Defence Colony and Lajpat Nagar too. He would claim we were college students and could not afford much. The excuse to take a room was my home was being painted and I was allergic to the smell and fumes of paint. It took us three days to finally book a room at an 'inn' on inner Ring Road in the Lajpat Nagar area. Adi negotiated an amazing deal as I paid just a bit over ₹1,000 per night for a really large room with an attached toilet. The room had a sofa and TV set too but was tacky, shouting out maintenance, but lived up to the price.

It was the month of March and I was on my last few days at *The Economic Times*, moving with Venu to a dot-com, managing news and research. As Venu said, the year 2000 was the beginning of a new century and it was time we did something new too. It was also the time of the dot-com boom which made the switch in job appealing, but not as exciting, new or fresh as a date with Samit.

Although my life had opened up to Ma, I had to keep this sojourn under wraps. So I told her that I was spending the weekend with Adi, and we may drive out to a place close to Delhi. Ma was happy I was doing things that I had not done before, like travelling out in the way Dilip and Duji did. She needed little reassurance of my safety as she had implicit trust in Adi.

The plan was this—meet Samit on a Friday evening, spend two nights with him and take it from there. I was expected to keep Adi updated to 'see how it goes' but also to alert him to any problem at the 'inn' or with Samit.

Uncertainties, living up to its meaning, crept in. Samit kept me waiting an hour on a road close to Paharganj, not returning the several calls I had made to him. Plans had changed. He gave no explanations when he did call back but said we were now meeting the next day, saying 'it's a promise'. I went back to the 'inn' for a short while but spent the night with Adi who cheered me up.

Samit did not break his promise. We drove to Colonel Kebabz in Defence Colony, bought some rolls and decided to carry them back to the room, on his suggestion. We got to the room and turned on the TV. He went for a shower and came out, slightly wet, with just a towel wrapped around his waist.

I was sitting on the three-seater sofa watching some inane TV show, with no interest. I asked him to sit next to me, moving a bit, not that he needed much room. He, however, decided to lie down, placing his head very close to my groin, so close, in fact, that he could feel my excitement, as it grew with every second. He looked at the TV and then at me, smiled, rubbed his hand on my chin and then on my cheeks.

He then guided me to the bed, taking off his towel, revealing his underwear and taut, small body. I lay down as he pulled off my T-shirt and then my trackpants. He then stretched himself over me, reaching my neck and kissing it. When he kissed my shoulder blades, I felt a current that was spectacular, surprising and delightful. He was all over me, giving my inexperienced body, a touch of ecstasy.

We didn't have sex though. He also did not indulge in a French kiss, just gracing my lips every now and then with a faint hint of his. But, none of this 'incompleteness' in sex—as defined by some friends—was of any relevance compared to everything else I felt with Samit when he was all over me.

Sleeping in his arms with my head on his shoulder, throughout the night, was peaceful. I woke up a few times to see his eyes shut, not disturbed by my movement. He looked like the most beautiful person I had ever seen, wishing for more time with him even if he just slept on my side.

I think I was falling in love when I saw him off the next day.

Chapter Twenty-six

WITHIN A FORTNIGHT, Samit was visiting home over the weekend. I had told Ma that he was someone I had met through Adi, giving my friendship with Samit some credibility.

Knowing the difference in our backgrounds, I was aware Samit was not very comfortable having dinner at home or meeting Ma. I was also not certain how Ma would respond to having someone over and in my room.

We stepped out for dinner, drove around the city till late so that by the time we reached home Ma would be asleep. She was already in bed after having done the most surprising thing of turning on the air conditioner in my room, making sure it was cool by the time we got home. She also left a note in the kitchen asking if Samit would have breakfast and if so, what should she prepare.

Samit and I, as hoped by me, got our hours of undisturbed intimacy. Over the next few weeks, this became a pattern for us. This 'something' with Samit is what I define as my first 'real' relationship. Adi and Dheeman were happy for me. Yet, two questions often came up: why had we not consummated our relationship and how come we had not yet experienced a French kiss in the truest way.

Adi wondered if Samit was gay or bisexual or just having a good time. I dismissed the questions and remarks saying it took time for love to grow and we had a lot of time ahead for this to happen. I, of course, did not admit that I was bothered by the question.

The next time we were in bed together, I did ask Samit why

he had avoided kissing me right from the beginning. He did not answer the question, but just placed himself above me and brought his face down, kissing and cuddling me amorously. For the next few minutes I was in bliss, my eyes closed, responding to his actions. When we stopped, he had a wicked smile, '*Ab khush* (Happy now)?'

I was soon venturing down the tiny streets of Paharganj where the passages, at times, were so small that only a single person could walk through. It was fascinating to see this part of Delhi that I had never thought of venturing into. We ate at dhabas close to his home with one of them becoming a favourite of ours as they served the most delicious palak paneer. There was also a niche-in-the-wall sweet shop that made some of the best pedas I had ever had. I used to bring some of this home and take it to office too.

As time passed and our interactions increased, we were off on a holiday first to Jaipur and later to Goa. He did not have the funds to cover the costs as most of his money had been invested in his recently opened travel company. So, I took charge on the understanding that he would pay back in due course of time.

The trip to Jaipur was a short one, two nights. But our visit to Goa was for a whole week. We swam in the sea the swimming pool and ate a whole lot of seafood. This was also the time when I broke my nine-year long period of vegetarianism, on his request.

One night, Samit tried to penetrate me wearing no condom, treating me in a rough manner. He was angry when I refused, ignoring what I had to say on safe sex, the use of condoms and HIV. I also did not like his aggression and told him that I would rather be on top. There was an angry outburst where he revealed he had slept with enough men and women to know what was safe and what wasn't.

I was scared by his anger and shocked by his sex life. I recall walking out of the hotel room to the beach, moist-eyed, staring at the darkness of the night. I was gone over an hour I think, and looked back frequently to see if Samit had come to find me, but he hadn't. He was asleep at the hotel, least bothered about me. I tried to sleep as well, sitting on a chair in the room and got into bed only in the early hours of the morning, recovering a bit looking at his calm face and beautiful body, lying next to me.

On returning to Delhi, he was busier than before, saying there were clients lining up and he had to attend to them. One weekend after another went by without us meeting and just two short phone calls, none of them made by him. Slowly, even that stopped. Finally, I went to his home twice finding it locked on both the occasions.

It was around then that a friend who had seen his photo implied he was philandering. I, of course, did not wish to believe this, as speculations of this sort were rife in the community. But then, where was he? His absence left me not knowing what to believe.

He resurfaced, after several days, first through short phone calls and then a long one with the final blow!

He was getting married—his mother had found a girl. The dowry was to cover loans as well as future business plans. I listened to him silently knowing that the end had come. 'We can still be together, meeting on and off, maybe not on all weekends,' he proposed and I declined, weeping, sure that it was either only the two of us or nothing at all.

Chapter Twenty-seven

THE ABSENCE OF Samit was like a big dark and deep hole. I lay in bed, crying, not knowing whom to speak to, randomly calling friends, telling them of the break-up, weeping, not listening to what some of them said, drowning them out with my howling.

I was in desperate need of support and someone to hold me. I had never cried like this or felt this helpless and lost. I did not know what could stabilize and bring me back to the person I was before I met Samit.

Adi suggested a solution that he practised after a futile attempt at having a relationship—go on a date and have fun.

'It is a release of sorts from the emotional stress one goes through at the time of separation. It also helps take the mind off the past, even if for a while,' he explained. 'What you and Samit shared was just sexual intimacy, there was nothing in common. He was your first and we all love intimacy; sometimes, we fall in love with it too,' Adi said leaving me pained and in thought. While I continued to believe that there was love, I also knew that at some level Adi was right. It had been the regularity of the weekend meetings, most of which ended with us sleeping together, that I treasured the most.

Still, I struggled to process Adi's counsel as this meant going on a shopping spree for flesh or meat, turning into a slut or a 'whore'—a word commonly used for gay men who had a prolific history of men they had slept with. Yet, since I was not fully ready to return to parties, I went online to a Yahoo gay chat room. I looked for profiles of men who sought love, relationships and life partners. I wanted to meet more than one person, maybe two or three, as it would give me options, a chance to know more people and hopefully not fall in love nearly instantly.

The first two dates ended quickly as they both wanted a sleepover to check out our sexual 'chemistry'. The third was a bit different. The picture he had shared online was of a person who was at least six to seven years younger than he was. Not knowing how to tell him that, I took him for a short drive, stopped at a tea stall and then said what I wished to. He admitted he had done wrong but said he was attracted to me and was aroused. 'It has been a while since I have had any fun,' he pleaded but I did not oblige.

These three outings, even though there was every reason for me to be disappointed, had made me a little stronger as I knew that I had a market. Over thirty was not yet over the hill.

As the monsoons dried up, farmhouse parties returned and so did I, after a bit of convincing by Adi, Venu and Chitra. I had not been to a party since I broke up with Samit.

It was an unusual party with the mix of music ranging from Dire Straits to Village People to Madonna to Abba to The Beatles to Suneeta Rao. This was like bliss for me—rock to disco to Hindi pop and no Bollywood with the exception of old film tracks being remixed. It was a busy dance floor, a near replica of the kind we saw in the film *Saturday Night Fever*; there were squares lit up in different colours, blinking on and off.

Crowded as it was, on one of the edges was the 'chocolate' boy, Promit—the man I had danced with at a private party in Green Park weeks before I met Samit. As I had noticed when I first met him he was neatly turned out wearing a pista green T-shirt and body-hugging jeans. And again, he was alone.

I took to the dance floor and moved my way towards him, inching closer and closer as Madonna's 'Like a Virgin' played. He responded with a smile, and inched forward as well. There was less than half a foot of distance between us. 'Wanna drink?' he asked and I nodded. We chatted at the bar about the music, what our jobs were and the weather, of course.

'There aren't many nice guys to talk to at these parties or in our community,' he said. I felt otherwise. 'I have not met many people but whoever I have, are pretty nice. I have such a good friend in Adi,' I said. 'The only reservation though is that many, or maybe the few I have met, seem to seek a one-night stand and I can't come to terms with that,' I added.

We were soon sitting at one of the benches slightly far from the dance floor, close to some bushes. There didn't seem to be anyone within listening distance. His mood changed and an expression of dejection took over as he looked down at the ground, saying nothing. I asked if he was okay, put my hand on his back and asked again, trying to get a glimpse of his face. 'It is a hard life, Sharif. Being in Delhi, going to work, looking after my mother,' he said in a soft and sad tone. 'I guess it is, I guess it is,' was what I said not knowing what his issues were. He remained silent for another couple of minutes and I maintained the quiet too.

But, he soon snapped out of that mood, got back on his feet saying we should enjoy the party, drink and dance, and meet our friends. 'Why waste an evening on something sad' was his way of explaining the sudden 'up' from the 'down' he was in.

By the time the party ended at 2 a.m. or so, we had danced with several people, forming a group that drove to the 24-hour Barista cafe at Krishna Hotel in Saket. During the course of the night, Promit, who was sitting at the other end of the table, having travelled in another car, would often look at me. As soon as our eyes would meet, he would smile and that smile seemed to acknowledge something that made me feel special even though I wondered what to make of it. No one had looked at me so often. At least no one whom I had noticed doing so!

It was about 4 in the morning by the time we left the cafe and headed to our respective homes. Promit did not ask to go home with me or ask me over. He was different after all, not seeking sex. This prompted me to suggest we meet again and he accepted.

But a couple of days went by without any message or a phone call from him. His silence was disturbing me. I wanted to see Promit again. I did not have the courage to ask him out one on one, like a date, as I was unaware of what he felt. Still, I called him and he sounded chirpy and ready to talk even though his pick-up from the call centre was about to reach. I told him that Adi and a few others were getting together on Saturday and asked if he would like to join in. 'I have no other plans. I am with you,' he said. I concealed my delight but boy was I waiting to see him again.

Promit sat in front, Adi and his friend, Karan, sat in the rear as we drove around Delhi with no agenda as such other than to listen to music and enjoy the open roads that the city had to offer. We actually had no places to go to other than a Barista cafe and Big Chill in East of Kailash, where we could sort of be ourselves. We drove from street to street, stopped to buy cigarettes and finally decided that Big Chill was where we could go. It was 10.30 p.m. by then, past closing time. But Adi got an assurance from Fawzia and Aseem—the owners—that they would allow us in.

Fawzia and Aseem were like vents of fresh air for us. Several friends I knew would head there for desserts and as the cafe expanded its menu, we were often seen grubbing in groups and some even coming in on a date. They never judged us or commented on what we liked or who we wished to go out with. That some of us were flamboyant to camp did not annoy them. The glitter that fell off many an over-glittered person never bothered them.

That night, the four of us were in a different zone, feeling very free and happy. All of a sudden, Promit stepped out of the cafe, just as I got up to visit the toilet. I returned, his phone was on the table but he had not come back. Aseem and Adi urged me to go out and check on him as he might be going through a difficult period.

He was sitting on the stairs that led up to the slightly raised ground floor of Big Chill. 'Are you okay?' I asked sitting down next to him. 'Sharif, just relax, it will be fine, just one of those personal issues,' he responded, explaining nothing. We sat there silently for a few minutes. He then stood up and helped me up. 'It has been one of the nicest evenings,' he said, looking straight at me, his hand reaching out for mine, his face a lot closer, close enough for us to kiss. And so we did.

Our eyes closed, possessed by that moment. To me, Promit had said everything without saying a word with that kiss which seemed to last probably half a minute. We were so taken in by that moment that neither of us noticed the cigarette and pan shop just beside the cafe. It was still open and there were a few people there. But fortunately no one seemed to have noticed us and if they did, they had not raised any objection.

I dropped him back home that night even though Adi and Karan stayed over at my place. I would have wanted to cuddle up with him in bed but I could not make myself ask him to stay-over.

Chapter Twenty-eight

THE PRESENCE OF Promit in my life added calm and certainty. He and I met often and spoke almost every night either when he was on his way to work or when he reached his workplace. This regularity of engagement was cementing my sexuality and the definitiveness of it, adding confidence to the person I was. I could now never imagine my sexuality being taken away or being confined to the norms or morality of society.

This is why I felt it necessary to share my secret with Rita mami and Ma's brother, Sudhir uncle, who had resumed their efforts to find me a wife. I somehow felt uncomfortable facing my aunt, as she was the one creating a dossier of girls, interacting with different families with daughters ready for marriage. She would be hurt and probably even angry if she'd known that I had been out and about for over a year.

So I met my uncle over drinks one evening using work as a pretext. As soon as we ordered drinks, my uncle took charge of the conversation. 'Your mami wants you to see these photos. Look at them and keep them if you want,' he said. I was staring at photos of three different girls—all prospects for marriage. All I was to do was pick one, mami would set up a meeting, I would meet the prospect and take it from there.

If a script was to go wrong, this was one of those moments it could have. I gently swept aside the photographs, pushing them to the corner of the table. I quickly looked away and ordered peanuts that would be good to munch on, nervously or calmly. 'I need to talk to you first,' I said.

Then, I came out to him. 'Mami does not need to look out or find anyone for me. She needs to know this, please,' I almost pleaded. My uncle had tears in his eyes and I could not look at him at that moment. I could see pain, disappointment and some shock. He finally spoke. 'What can I say. If my sister is okay with it and you are fine, I have nothing much to say,' he responded. 'Though Rita will be surprised,' he said. 'She was so eager and sure to find you a life partner who would make you happy. You know she loves you like her son,' he added.

I ordered another round of drinks—I think we both needed it and told him of my life so far. I let him know of the farmhouse parties and that they were hosted hardly a few kilometres away. I told him of my failed relationship as well as the existence of Promit.

He didn't seem very interested in these details as perhaps the reality of a gay nephew was still sinking in.

Around 11 that night, I got a call on my mobile phone. It was Rita mami. She said, 'Sharif, you need not have been so scared. You could have spoken to me too.'

'We are with you. If I am concerned about anything it is that it can be lonely. I don't know of any gay relationships and whether they last. What would you do when Ma is gone and we too.' Saying so much, my aunt left me feeling loved and cared for, not being judged at all for who I had come out to be. She even promised to talk to my cousins, her daughters—Bijoya and Purabi—who grew into being more loving sisters than they already were.

I slept off very happy, sharing the news with Adi first and then Chitra and Venu, the next morning. Then I told Promit hoping that I could introduce him to Rita mami one day to let her know that there were some gay couples, and we were one of them. I was very hopeful of Promit and me making it work. While Adi was supporting and encouraging of our affection for each other, he also kept cautioning me to take things as they came, day by day. This was exactly the counsel that even Rita mami gave me when I told her about Promit some days later.

However, I felt he was a solid guy. He worked hard and the results were there to be seen. He was being designated trainer which was a step up in the hierarchy at his place of work. This meant more money and control over his schedule since a trainer did not need to be at work every night servicing the US or the UK markets.

He had started coming home on Saturdays. He met Ma, they spoke a lot and he seemed to respect her, admiring her openness to him and us. He wished there were more mothers like her and he told me the several times.

I met his mother too as a friend and not as anyone special. His mother spoke Bengali and a bit of Hindi. I knew a few words in Bengali and my Hindi was better but still distant from correct usage of words and grammar. It was enough, though, to get a conversation going with his gentle mother.

He also had a sister who was studying then and seemed to be aiming for a job similar to Promit's. He was very protective of her and generally acted as the man of the house after he had lost his father about a year before. His father had been a government official which is why they had a quarter in RK Puram, very close to Munirka.

As much as he loved his family, Promit was never happy living the life he had. The size of his home, the dark streets that led to it, the seepage in the walls—all of it bothered him. The fact that he could speak English fluently while his mother and sister could not made him feel superior to them and almost disconnected with their history which he was a part of.

This, naturally, made the new position at work and the hike in salary a significant development in his career. It was a 30 per cent jump in his take home, excluding perquisites and bonuses. If he did more than the regular shift, this would reflect in his final monthly salary as well as the annual assessments.

To celebrate this milestone, Promit was soon packing for a vacation in London. This was scheduled days after 9/11, an attack that shook the world. He had just mentioned the trip as we saw the aircrafts crash into the World Trade Center in New York. I did not want him to go. I was getting so used to meeting him and having him around. He did not have a return date too which kind of left me in a bit of limbo. 'I will be back, don't worry,' he said leaving things open and unsure.

As usual, I turned to Adi wondering what I should make of this new development. He asked me multiple questions: were Promit and I dating, seeing each other or were we boyfriends. I was confused. What was seeing each other? 'I see him, he sees me, we are together. Is there more to it?' I asked.

What more could there be? We had slept together, been out with our families but maybe that was not enough to give our relationship a status.

Chapter Twenty-nine

I HAD HOPED Promit would ask me to travel with him but he didn't. He was so absorbed by the thought of flying out of India, the costs and the thrill of it being a hard-earned trip, a reward of sorts that nothing seemed to cross his mind as his departure date got closer.

I dropped him to the airport and left him with a tearful send off, 'crying like a baby', as he said. The tears never stopped, not even in the car as the cassette played one love song after another—Enrique's 'Escape', a song that we claimed as ours, followed by Bryan Adams' 'When You're Gone', a song that referred to the realization of love resulting from the absence of a special person, the state that I was in.

I had no phone number to call him at. He was to give that to me later once he had settled in London. He wasn't regular on emails either. And I did not hear from him for three days in a row. I was getting edgier by the hour. I toyed with all the options I had and the only answer to the predicament was to fly off to London and see him there, only if I had his coordinates.

As luck would have it, he did send me an email with his phone number and address, four days after he left Delhi. I replied with my plans to fly in, a decision he welcomed. 'That is quick, it is going to be fun,' he replied.

I discussed this with Ma and spoke to Uma masi who had moved to London in 1988 to ask if I could stay with her for a few days.

Then, I sought permission from Venu who cleared my leave as the stories around 9/11 had died down too. I also informed Adi who was a bit surprised. 'Don't let this trip revolve around him, please as it can be very disappointing. If this visit is just for him, your days and nights will depend entirely on his schedules, moods and commitments and that can leave anyone on tenterhooks,' he said. 'And you have family there, Duji, Masi, don't forget that,' he added.

Uma masi and her son, Aftab, lived in Waylett Place, part of the Wembley area in London where many South Asian families lived. Aftab was in a relationship with Minal, someone I was yet to meet. My other cousin, Mehtab, was married to Rajiv and resided in Wimbledon. She was an advocate and Rajiv was a criminal psychologist.

Mehtab and I had a very special bond. I guess we spent more time together, chatting and playing silly games as kids that led to a stronger connect than I had with Aftab. He was much younger and a bit of a terror when he was a kid, at times even scaring me with his pranks. But now he was a smart man in the world of marketing.

As I boarded my Virgin Airline flight for London, it dawned on me that Uma masi was not yet aware of my sexuality. I had only told Mehtab who in turn had informed Aftab. If Promit were to come over, Masi needed to know who he was. This automatically put my coming out to her at the top of my agenda, ticking it off my list soon after I reached London and their home.

'Masi, we need to talk. You've often asked me about a girl, getting married. But I've got to tell you, I am gay and a wedding is not going to happen!'

Even before I could tell her that Ma, knew I was gay and had accepted me, she burst into tears. She blamed herself. She wondered why I had not told her earlier and asked more than once if I was sure of my sexuality.

I had not anticipated such a dramatic response. Why was she

to take any blame for who I was, I wondered. Masi said, 'After you lost your father, I should have spent more time with you. Had I done that, I think things would have been different.'

She believed life then was not easy for Ma. Yet, how could that have changed anything?. How could Masi's presence have changed my sexuality? What was it to do with us losing Pa very early in our lives, my life in particular, and have a bearing on my sexuality?

'Masi, my sexuality has nothing to do with any of these circumstances: whether you were there or not, or the timing of Pa's death,' I tried to explain but her tears did not stop and she murmured several times that it was her fault and that I was 'too young' to understand.

Not knowing what else to say, I merely apologized.

Chapter Thirty

THE NEXT MORNING things were back to normal, except Masi had puffy eyes, giving away how sleepless she had been. In her interaction with me, she wasn't any different from the person I had known prior to our conversation the night before. Her love and care never diminished, in fact, she was curious to know about the person I had come chasing to London. 'Go spend time with him but tell me more about what's happening,' she had said.

Promit and I walked the streets of Central London from Piccadilly to Covent Garden, spent hours at Soho and even headed down to South Banks, an area that my brother, Duji, spent a lot of his free time at, just like he did at Soho whenever he had a chance. Another favourite was a small muffin place at Covent Garden just opposite the multi-storey HMV store (which is no longer there) where I always lost track of time.

On one such afternoon, Duji, Promit and I met. I could never tell what my brother felt about Promit as he carried on a conversation on London, the culture, arts and architecture. Duji did ask a few questions like where he lived, where we had met and about the origin of Promit's accent—it was a mix of American and Indian and British, dropping hints of each every now and then. There was, of course, a bit of sarcasm in that question as Duji was one of those South Asians who retained the tone, style and accent that they had prior to moving to the UK, emphasizing their sense of identity and origin.

We were to go to visit Duji and Peggy at their home in Greenwich a few days later but before that a large dinner had been planned at a Central London restaurant. This dinner included my childhood friend, Nitin, who was living in Ealing with his wife, Rachna, Duji and Peggy, Aftab with Minal and Promit and I. 'This is a night out for couples,' said Duji.

'My boyfriend and I, out with other couples! This is lovely!' Promit said almost gurgling over the phone when I called to inform him of the plans. That moment was the high point of my trip to London. His statement—my boyfriend and I—repeated in my head again and again. Smiling privately, I saw this as an accomplishment and progression in our relationship which had no status or grade when I had left Delhi earlier that month. I was itching to tell someone but there was no one to share this titbit with. Everyone in London had already assumed he was my boyfriend, connecting my chase to London as love between two people, a couple in a relationship.

Promit and I finally got to spend a night together. This was at Peggy and Duji's home—a large nineteenth-century building with a huge fireplace. The living area was a sizeable one, enough to fit a couple of bedrooms into. There was a large sofa, antique-looking, rugs on the floor and a few modern-day mattresses, jarring against the sense of age that romantically defined that home and space. The room was dimly lit; it took a few seconds to adjust to the light, most of which came from the wood that was crackling in the fireplace. The wine was warm too—mulled wine I think—something we desperately needed as we had just returned from a very cold night out at Heaven's, a gay disco somewhere near Trafalgar Square.

As Duji and Peggy wound up for the night, we remained in the living area, lying on the mattresses, tucked under a quilt, enjoying the warmth of the fire and each other.

Promit was keen to tell me something as we lay almost lip-locked. He had been very stressed over the past few years, particularly after he lost his father, something he had indicated earlier too. The odd hours at work and just being cooped up in a different time zone, the stress was telling on him, he said. 'Sometimes I can't get it up, Sharif,' he said, not using the words sexual disorder or erectile dysfunction. 'Can't get it up as in?' I asked not sure if it was a problem or the chemistry between us.

I knew he had been aroused on a few occasions when we had hugged each other but I was also aware from some reports online that there was a section of gay men who suffered from the fear of performance failure. There was, as on everything, two views on this subject since erectile dysfunction was not exclusive to gay men. Viagra, after all, was for all men.

Promit had anyway started consulting a doctor in Delhi in the hope of fixing this. I could see the embarrassment writ on his face. I held him tight, saying that just being with him, in his arms, was satiating and that he would be well soon.

Chapter Thirty-one

IN A FEW days, I returned to Delhi feeling a lot more certain and sure about 'us' than when Promit had boarded his flight for London. I got back five days before him and as life is, we both returned to our respective routines of work and home. There was a difference now—we started going out regularly to private parties and coffee shops as a couple.

The occasional weekday off for him, if a Tuesday, meant he and I could attempt an evening of dancing at Someplace Else at the Park Hotel. On one such Tuesday, we pulled Adi out. He had only recently broken off with Dheeman. It was one of those rare nights where even Nishit, the film-maker, was also there. With him, there was a playwright from Nagaland and a couple of others.

We spoke briefly as we had met only occasionally at film festivals or some farmhouse party. I learnt that he was on the verge of starting a new film or had some project in mind. We did not get into the details as the place and decibel levels were hardly conducive to such conversations. He, in any case, was being bombarded with questions from others.

Promit, Adi and I left a little after 1 a.m. I dropped both of them before returning home a bit past two in the morning. The next morning my phone received a flurry of messages. To my dismay and shock, Nishit had died in a car crash! As I reached office, I checked agency reports that said five young people were killed in a car crash around 2 a.m. They were heading southwards, down the same route we had taken a little earlier, crossing Lodhi Road. It was a drunken truck driver that smashed into the Maruti car that Nishit was in, breaking the vehicle to bits.

The gay community, I recollect, was stunned. Nishit was not just an activist but also an icon to many. His documentary, *Summer in My Veins*, was part of our movement. Nishit had become a voice for us, writing numerous articles in papers, speaking at forums and allowing his film to be shown at different festivals since it debuted in 1999. He wasn't a Siddharth Gautam who joined the AIDS Bhedbhav Virodhi Andolan (ABVA) after returning from Yale at the end of the 1980s or an Ashok Row Kavi, but he was who he was, mattering to our time and the overall movement at that juncture. There was little doubt that he would have contributed a lot more had his life not been cut short on that tragic day of April 2002.

Several of us gathered that weekend and talked about his sudden death, his contribution to the movement and what it was to come out and live in India where even urban, so-called progressive societies were nothing but regressive. Several friends had remained silent about their sexuality even in industries termed liberal and open such as advertising. I remember sharing stories I had gotten to know of.

According to an account from Jhelum Ratna, my sister-in-law who was married to my first cousin Anand (my father's nephew), there were many gay men who remained silent. 'Someone we all respected died young, of a heart attack,' she said stressing that her fraternity believed it was caused by the stress of living a dual life. I shared what the Indi-pop star, Suneeta Rao, once told me, that the situation was so dark and bleak where even in the world of music and arts, men and women had concealed their sexuality, fearing the worst in terms of jobs and society.

Yet, there were also people like Subhashish whose mother had accepted him. Another friend, who was once a counsellor at Humrahi, was also out and happy at home. There were, however, less than a handful of such stories which meant that being yourself, openly, was being valiant and not just brave.

If there was anyone who put things into context at that time, it was Saleem. 'How can anyone come out and talk about their sexuality easily when even masturbation puts many—straight people too—on a guilt trip,' he said referring to conversations he had when he was a counsellor in Delhi.

Promit was of the view that living in India was a miserable thought as leading a normal life safely and without fear was not possible. He would often say he was an international citizen and not an Indian one. 'I can cross borders and live anywhere but here,' he said posing the thought as a question to me. I had never thought about this and I saw no reason to leave my mother back in a city that was unsafe for women. We, my mother and I, were also so used to our routines that overlapped gently every day, be it the early morning rush of doorbells and domestic tasks or the dinner in her room with our meal placed on a tiny black trolley that my brothers and I gave her on her fiftieth birthday.

Yet, Promit's story and life were different. He strongly believed in his view and repeated it often, and I did not realize that it was an indication of things to come.

The relationship started to slip and friends in our very intimate community told me he was sleeping around. Some claimed he was seen walking with a 'white' man in Vasant Vihar. I disregarded the chatter, strongly believing in the love we had.

While the truth of who this 'white' person was (assuming he existed) or who all he may have slept with (which I gathered was true) was not known to me, Promit became more and more elusive and unavailable, leading to a final break-up—something that he wanted desperately. He soon moved to Germany and later got married and settled down with a local, pretty much taking India off his radar, barring the few visits, I heard, he made to see his mother and sister.

I was peeved and hurt but the gradual demise of our relationship made the pain more manageable. I had enough people around me who were critical of Promit, claiming he was unreliable and a cheat. Their comments were like support for me. However, while the issue of commitment, honesty and truth were matters that bothered me initially, in time I realized he was silently repressed in his own family.

On the one hand, he was the good son, working hard and paying most of the bills at home. But at the same time, the other him had a deep desire of being someone else. He aspired for greater income and to have his own space. His mother, however, had neither seen much space nor the kind of lifestyle he wished to have, so she could never even think of it and he could never tell her.

He was one amongst many other gay men who wanted to leave India and restart life in safer surroundings that did not interfere with one's sexual identity. The combination of reasons may have differed but the general narrative and distress were the same.

I remember a journalist who had once shared a room with Adi, had packed his bags and left for France just like that. He is now living with his partner. A fashion stylist I knew had moved to San Francisco, an engineer friend was in Bangkok, a film-maker had moved to New York and so many others were in London, Amsterdam, Sydney, Berlin and so on. Even Kathmandu was an option.

No doubt, any of us would be second-class citizens in Europe or the West but that could hardly be a hindrance for those who made such a choice when in any case none of us were first class in our own country.

With Promit gone, I slumped a bit, landing in the arms of Chitra, crying. I had lost Samit, failed to be with Dheeman and now was without Promit. There was a sense of failure as well as a regret that I came out late. 'I either misread things or do not comprehend them. I seem to be slow off the block,' I remember telling Chitra.

Her view though was simple and pointed. 'Imagine what it would have been like if you had come out years ago. The world would have been more hostile, there may not have been any Naz Foundation or group meetings and probably the world would have been far more complex, denying you support from friends and family—something you have now.'

Venu felt I had to slow down and meet more people. 'Try and figure out the variety, what you like, what you don't,' he said implying I wasn't giving myself any time to do so, resulting in troughs and peaks, one after another. 'These ups and downs are not worth it. It impacts you emotionally and mentally, makes you vulnerable and can come in the way of your career and responsibilities at home and work,' he stated simply.

Chapter Thirty-two

I DECIDED TO put one foot on the brake when it came to love and relationships and the other on the accelerator, opening up my mind and soul to an ever-changing gay world.

I scanned gay chat sites such as Guys4Men (which was acquired by Planet Romeo in 2009) and gaydar.uk (which soon seemed to die out) and became a regular at gay nights hosted at a bar in the Chanakyapuri area called Pegs N Pints (referred to as PNP by us). This outlet replaced Someplace Else as our weekly Tuesday hub. Farmhouse parties had died out, threatened by raids by police and excise officials and violent intrusions by straight men.

PNP, however, turned into a temple of sorts. The dark, dingy place with a spiral staircase to the mezzanine level, from where we would view just about everyone, was divine for us. It wasn't rare to find partygoers spilling onto the pavement and street because the place was always packed. There was something magnetic about the venue; it showcased a certain invincibility for itself and us, ensuring that any place that tried to have a gay night on Tuesday was bound to fail.

What was quite apparent at that time was the absence of the lesbian community. I was told that lesbians in any case hardly stepped out but I also heard that they felt threatened by the boisterous behaviour of some gay and bisexual men as well as male sex workers who offered their services not knowing they were lesbians!

Slowly but surely, the presence of cross-dressers was on the rise, working their way into the party scene, ignoring the phobia that a large number previously held. I remember how some men would change their clothes in the toilet, coming out in a different avatar, wearing what 'women wore', facing lewd comments and hostility. I would look at them curiously, wondering why they wore such clothes, never reaching out to them or being abusive.

As I freed myself a bit, I started hosting parties too. I would cook, arrange inexpensive alcohol and soft drinks. I would put together dance music and allow my friends to bring others too not knowing then that the 'others' could be a man someone just picked up from Nehru Park or a hulk connected with for the first time on a gay chat site. The open home and conversations gave me some kind of recognition amongst the small group I had gotten to know. A few such new acquaintances even started following my work as a researcher-cum-reporter working under Venu at the dot-com.

It was around that time that I broke a report related to a large Indian corporation and its funding structure. While the report appeared on our website, I think it was also used or referred to by other media. The story created an unexpected furore in the political circles.

What happened a few days later was as unexpected as the controversy the story generated. One night as I was heading back home, around 8 p.m., I was assaulted by a group of three men, who knocked me around for 30 or 40 minutes. Not that I recall every detail but I can recount some parts of this event that shook me out of my sense of security.

When I regained consciousness, my files of papers including those related to the report I had written were strewn all over. Many of the confidential documents were missing. I tried to reach out to my phone and spotted it near the front right tyre of my car on the inner side, below the engine. My body was aching and at that moment I had no idea where the pain was coming from, as it seemed to be all over.

I suddenly felt something wet, it was my blood. My pants were partly down, my underwear too, not from the front though. I turned to the right to find a wooden stick which had traces of blood on one end and a cloth wrapped on the other. It was only then that I realized that the stick had entered me during the course of the attack.

The first hit was directed at my diaphragm, the second at my right knee. I remembered one of the men saying, '*Humko pata hai aap kya pasand karte ho, toh maza aayega apko* (We know what you like. You will enjoy this.)' Evidently, the idea of maza or fun was to have that stick pushed up, inside me. They knew about my sexuality, I deduced.

I finally managed to get myself up. I had tears but could not cry. I guess it was shock. I pulled out tissues from the car, wet them with drinking water that I had in my car and wiped my arms and then my rear. Barring some bruises and a slight tear on my pants, I didn't look like a person who had gone through a sexual assault of the nature that I just had. This was the only saving grace as I did not have to tell Adi what had happened when I headed to his home that night, for a late dinner. I told him that the scratches and the dirt marks on my clothes were resultant of a fall.

As the night progressed, my body ached and I seemed to see visuals—mostly shadows of the three men. I even imagined the wielding of the stick. That image comes back to haunt me till today as I make attempts to be a bottom or experiment with my sexual role as a 'versatile'. Any entry into that area always leads to me tightening my muscles, expecting pain.

I did not file a complaint as I thought the best way to deal with it was silence. If I told Ma, she would have been paranoid, probably assuming that I was always at risk because I was gay. I doubted the police could have done much and the case would have kept the incident alive, making a closure of any kind impossible.

If the media got wind of it, it would have been front-page news, exposing my family and the gay community too!

Till now, I am not sure if it was a hate crime in the true sense or a retaliation by a corporate that had a strong intelligence system, aiming to hit me where it hurt most. What I know though is that it denied me years of mental and emotional peace and fuller sexual intimacy with partners who could well have been my lovers, had I been able to allow consummation with me as the 'bottom', exploring my sexual versatility.

Chapter Thirty-three

I WENT OFF the gay party circuit unsure if I could face up to the prospects of anything physical. I had once called a masseur who used to massage every part of my body but I froze when his hands touched my private parts, leaving me cold and sweaty. I had looked at myself in the mirror noticing how the colour of my skin had paled.

It was months before I could revisit the gay scene but that came after a lot of convincing that life had to carry on. I also told myself that sitting back and denying myself my own life was letting the sexual offenders win.

What ultimately got me going was a recollection of a conversation with Ma on how she had adjusted to Delhi, the lack of respect for women, the remarks on her art and sense of design and the comments on her character by people who were not so close but not so distant either. She said that she took things as they came and moved ahead with what she felt was her priority rather than ponder on the problems. In fact, even when I came out, she went with the flow rather than allowing a conflict to erupt at that point because she was more concerned about me dealing with my sexuality.

So, yes, I was back! Nothing much had changed in the small gay world of ours in those months of my absence. PNP was as busy as ever, men were clinging to men, kissing, dancing, cross-dressing, all of that had remained. My eyes had adjusted not just to the dim lights of the nightclub but also to spotting men. On one such night I saw a group of three young men walking in just as the lights were turned on and the night was coming to a close. They were perhaps the best of what I had ever seen in a long while.

I was with Vinay (a friend who went on to become very dear to me) on that night. He was a designer and part owner of a luxury cosmetic brand. He knew all three, introducing me to them one by one. There was Ron who is now a top fashion stylist, Arjun who currently is the country head of a European luxury fashion brand and Jonathan who is in the public relations field at this point, having dabbled in journalism earlier. When I met them, they were still finding their feet, so to speak, in the city and their career.

Ron and Jonathan were from Manipur and Arjun from Lucknow. My eyes were on the two Manipuri men. Their oriental, Asian looks had caught my fancy. Even Vinay had a similar preference and neither of us showed any special interest in Arjun. I learnt that Vinay had a consistent attraction for North Easterners, and was a Rice Queen—a term used for men who were attracted to oriental or Mongoloid features.

The conversation between Ron, Jonathan and Arjun was strange. It started with what and how much they had drunk that night, to where they had been and their plans later, after leaving PNP. 'Take one of them home,' Vinay said jokingly. But they turned and looked at me, almost hoping I would say yes. I chose to get their—Ron's and Jonathan's—phone numbers instead, to invite them for a party I was organizing that weekend.

Ron did not respond to my invitation and Jonathan kind of played hard to get. But he turned up, saying it was a surprise, which it was. He was the oldest of the three, more familiar with Delhi and a student at Delhi University, living in the North Campus area. He was still getting a hang of the city and was not someone who regularly went to parties, and definitely not alone. Still, he wasn't averse to testing the waters. 'It may be too late for me to head back, it is a long way from North Campus,' he told me an hour after having arrived.

In short, he wanted to stay the night, a request I was not going to turn down.

He and I danced a lot, till the party ended around 4 a.m. At that time, I still had the slim single bed and a mattress for a second person sleeping over. Young, full of energy and someone familiar with sensual dancing, Jonathan put up a show, something like a strip tease, taking off each bit of clothing and accessory one by one, leaving only his underwear on. I was both amazed and amused as this 'show' unfurled. We talked, cuddled, kissed and seemed to have a chemistry that was youthful and warm, keeping us in bed till almost midday.

Jonathan and I stayed in touch over the phone and then started to meet regularly. There was an affection for sure between the two of us—a familiarity that came with our on and off nights together. I was fascinated by his youthfulness and innocence. And he enjoyed music, in fact some of the bands he listened to were among my favourites.

In a few weeks, we were meeting so often that he blurted the word love and that he was looking for more. I, however, was hesitant and non-committal. I was not ready for anything concrete as I had not forgotten the wise counsel of Venu that I must meet more people. I was also enjoying the nights at PNP and a new kind of liberation that allowed me a Jonathan and probably some others as and when I wished. Besides, as I told myself, and Jonathan too, he was just nineteen years old and must see the world before committing to a relationship.

Sweet as he was, he was probably as mixed up as I had been when I had first met Samit. These suggestions that I was making to him were oddly, the wisdom that I had lacked back in 1999 when I had come out. We settled, for an open relationship, even though Jonathan preferred monogamy. We had a few rules—we could have multiple partners but none to be repeated. Kissing was also not allowed. These were norms that we recalled being a part of an agreement between Brian and Justin in the series *Queer as Folk*. However, since we kept meeting so often, there was no scope or time to sleep with another person, or even feel the desire to do so.

I, in fact, was even a bit indulgent, taking him to places he wished to go to or stopping by his home in Amar Colony (where he had moved to) late at night when he wanted to see me. We also went on a short weekend trip to Jaipur. He also had a wish—a fetish actually—to see me in a suit.

Even though I was now a director on the board of Integral PR while running the research firm that Venu had quit before moving back to *The Economic Times*, I rarely ever followed the corporate norm of formal wear. But there was that one night where I was left with no other option as it was an event at The Oberoi, with a stated dress code, celebrating ten years of one of our most prestigious clients.

On my way to the event, I decided to stop by Jonathan's home, parking between Lady Shri Ram College and my school, FAPS. He was thrilled beyond words. He got into the car and looked at me, delighted. He even suggested that I should wear a suit more often and use the tie collection I had inherited from my father. Within minutes, he stretched over to kiss me, placing his hand on my thigh and feeling me up.

We may have been together not more than ten minutes when suddenly I spotted a light reflecting in the side rear-view mirror. Just as I pushed Jonathan away, there was a wooden stick banging at the window. There was a policeman right there asking me to step out, shining a torch in my face.

I got out of the car and then Jonathan was asked to step out too. There was a second cop who held Jonathan by his arm, directing him to the high boundary wall of FAPS. The police claimed they knew what we were up to and that we had violated the law.

They had my car keys and had taken all my business cards threatening to call my office. I told them to come home, take whatever they wished but to let go of Jonathan and me. I did try and place an argument claiming we had done nothing and were only talking but they weren't buying it. I was asked if I was married and if not, why was I single, trying to profile me saying, '*isliye woh ladka* (that's why that boy)', hinting at my sexuality and that Jonathan was a prostitute and I his client. But that Jonathan and I shared how we knew each other—our names and addresses too—calmed the policemen a bit who changed tack playing the game of cold and hot cop.

Ultimately, I knew we had to settle this matter with whatever money I had. Yet, at that time, both Jonathan and I were palpitating, hearing our hearts pound, scared to bits. The large wooden stick in the hand of the policemen was ominous as they made gestures that reminded me of my recent past.

We got off lucky unlike many other gay men who had been through sexual assault and false cases being filed against them. After this incident, Jonathan and I never kissed each other in the car or even hugged in any public place.

Jonathan thought I had been very brave and had saved him even though I was trying to settle a matter to the benefit of both of us. Being his 'saviour' led him to assume we had a far greater bond than ever—something that had to see him through his whole life and that I was his and no one else's. That led him to seek more and more time from me even if it was quantity over quality.

It made things difficult as he wanted a regular account of where I was, who I was speaking to or meeting. Even if I was with Vinay, our common friend, he would make a dozen calls asking what we were speaking about. He hounded me on my office direct line too and made late night calls on the landline number at home if I did not answer his calls on the mobile.

This drew Ma into our relationship as she once picked up the call. She knew there was a problem and I admitted it too. 'Well, you led him on, didn't you,' Ma posed a question while commenting on the person I had been and the person I had become.

I carried that guilt as Jonathan and I headed for a break-up. This time I cried not because we were parting ways but because he was crying and for whatever reason, I had never wanted to see tears in his eyes, but now I was the cause for his crying.

Our paths did cross many times over the years and that friendship we shared still exists. Till date, we remain civil and that is something we could both be proud of. He, I believe, still has a soft corner for me, thinks of me as Brian and himself as Justin, continuing in an endless open relationship just like in *Queer as Folk*.

Chapter Thirty-four

I KNEW OF fag hags and their interest in the lives of gay men. I never, however, thought that a straight man would ever be curious about a gay man's life. One of our closest family friends, Lohit, often referred to as the fourth boy at home by Ma since he had spent so much time with us being very close to Dilip and Duji, had just learnt that I was gay.

Apparently, Duji had told him of my recent relationship with Jonathan when Lohit asked if I had marriage on my mind or had dropped it altogether. Driving through Delhi on an assignment with the army, he dropped in to check on Ma—as he always did—and then to chat with me. A long chat it was, as he for the first time entered my personal life.

He asked, did I hold hands of a person I was in love with? Was it special to be in each other's arms, not always wanting to have sex? Have I gone on dates? Do you watch films together? Are there common interests that lead to bonding? Would you want to live with your lover?

As I said yes to almost every question, Lohit kept saying 'just like us' in an innocent yet excited manner at discovering the commonalities. He was trying to draw parallels, not sure what gay men were about. All he had heard was about promiscuity in the gay world and that there was perhaps no value for love and relationships.

I recall doing a couple of rounds of coffee while telling Lohit that bonding was a problem not because of who we were but because of circumstances.

'Think of it—can a gay person be openly gay at work? A heterosexual doesn't even have to think about it. He is free to talk and explore common ground and interests with another person of her or his liking. They spend hours together at a workplace even if in different departments, often enjoying common friends—none of whom they need to find. That kind of freedom allowed Sonu and Dilip to meet,' I explained.

'Similarly, there were no schools or colleges that provided an ecosystem that normalized the possibility of same-sex attractions. Imagine, Nitin and Rachna's love story began in school!' I gave another example.

'Even residential complexes and colonies are dominated by the acceptance of love between opposite sexes, neither of whom have any awkwardness of being themselves. Rahul met his wife in Gulmohar Park! And for Duji, it was in the world of academics that he met Peggy.'

When any of 'us' meet, we snatch or grab the only commonality we have, that is our sexuality. In a way, many of us run the risk of falling in love with lust, missing the other dimensions of a person that are integral to cementing a partnership. 'But you know what, even as we know this, we don't mind erring time and again because it is far better than having no one!' I concluded.

'Well, at least you aren't forced into arranged marriages,' he quipped, trying hard to lighten the mood. 'Small mercies,' I responded in a very dry tone.

Lohit wondered if we would ever have a more open system and a law that would allows us to be who we were and even a classified to an arranged marriage system. 'Right now I can't even write under my own name,' I said, smiling, revealing my pen-name to him—Bharat I. Sharma.

Bharat came from our country's name, the 'I' stood for India and Sharma I thought was an easy and common surname I had heard across the cities I had lived in. I picked such a name, as it represented my thought that being gay should be as common as a Sharma is in an India or a Bharat. It was also the name used by Anita Jain in her bestselling book, *Marrying Anita*, where she describes me as her guide into the gay community and the nights at PNP.

In one of my interactions at her friend's home, a few days after meeting Lohit, I was once again faced with multiple questions and observations. That friend thought just about every other Indian man was gay. She reached that conclusion observing men holding hands walking down the streets and even the way men danced together at weddings and discos. 'It is not a reflection of sexuality, it is just how Indian men bond,' I told her and then referred to Sufal who did not draw lines when it came to sex maintaining fluidity

Prita, another friend of hers, asked me the most stunning question. 'What does anal sex feel like? Is it like an enema?' 'Why?' I asked, adding, 'It is a bit personal.' Apparently, she was hoping to experiment with sex with someone new in her life. She claimed there were other girls like her, implying that the idea of sex itself was changing.

Till then I thought 'carnal' sex or 'unnatural' sex, as Section 377 puts it, was exclusive to gay and bisexual men! Of course, I was learning new things from the world that appeared to be changing.

Chapter Thirty-five

PRITA AND I met and spoke often. I guess she felt more liberated and safe with people like me as we were also testing the waters and boundaries that society had set. She had reached an understanding with her boyfriend that if he wasn't up to experimenting how they had intercourse, the option of a third person had to be considered—she was knocking fidelity off its pedestal by having a polygamous relationship.

Again I assumed this was common in the gay world only and my only experience of such an arrangement were with Jonathan even if it were a half-baked effort.

It was on a visit to Bangkok that year that I got to see it working and understood its importance. My favourite place in that city was the oldest gay bar in the region—Telephone Bar. One of the owners then, Wayne Waterson, an Australian and fifty-eight years old at that time, was seeing a young Thai boy, who was most likely in his mid-20s. They loved each other deeply and it was evident as I saw it grow over the years.

What many scorned at, I recall, was that it was an open relationship questioning or challenging their idea of love and commitment. Some also commented on the age difference between the two—something I was faced when Jonathan and I were together. However, what I learnt from Wayne was that love is much stronger than a possession or merely the physical. He argued that at no point when he slept with someone else, did his care and affection for his partner ever diminish. This is what his partner told me too, as he slipped into the arms of Wayne.

Given that sex by itself hardly sees a relationship through and it takes all kinds of bonding—that of the mind, values, common interests and even children in some cases—why hanker over the physical aspects and make it so integral to love like it were the glue to keep two people together.

As Wayne put it, we were influenced from the single idea of a relationship built around the institution of marriage. This is what has been sold to us as romance and a 'perfect' commitment through advertisements, films and Valentine's Day. 'I mean, very simply the idea of a romantic dinner is almost just one—candlelit. You give flowers and expensive rings and so on. It means love and romance need these props? Absurd, isn't it?'

The challenge posed to marriage as an institution comes from polygamy and the genuine possibility of multiple children and their security—financial and emotional. 'That is a realistic problem but then what are condoms and birth control for,' he remarked adding, 'and as far as we go, where are we producing kids?' True, I agreed.

Soon, I was testing polygamy in its truer sense and age gap in long distance relationships over the years with Thai men and a Malay boy. Some of the men were 16 to 20 years younger than me. At no point were any of the relationships defined monogamous. What was stated was that we were together at least when we were in the same city.

While the first of the Thai encounters was with a masseur who later became a gym trainer, the second worked in the retail industry and the third, a Malay, was studying medicine in Bengaluru. I always believed that given the age difference, the levels of energy, excitement and libido in addition to the distance, it was unfair to expect any of my boyfriends to be trapped in fidelity. They would have to cheat and lie to live their lives, so why force either of us into a state of guilt?

As it was, each of these relationships never worked out. The masseur felt we were chalk and cheese and he never liked Delhi. For that relationship to work, he felt I had to move to Bangkok. The other Thai was in perpetual financial need with almost no other connect between ourselves. The Malay was moving back to his country and we were certain that the added distance would be an impediment. What we were left with was a friendship that still exists.

Chapter Thirty-six

MY FIRST TRIP to Bangkok, when I had met Wayne, left me surprised and delighted with the openness towards the community and its visibility in day-to-day life. Not only were gay men just about everywhere, so were lady boys and lesbians. That you could be yourself, out on a date, off to a hotel room or just strolling in a park, without the glare of people, was probably the most liberating experience of that city.

Departing from Bangkok left me in tears as I flew back to Delhi wondering why I even lived there. I knew it was Ma and the convenience of familiarity and a career that held me back from any move out of the city. To say I was frustrated was an understatement.

Within days the city was struck by the murder of Pushkin Chandra, a gay man who lived some three hundred metres from my home. While we as a community were shocked, the way the media reported the ghastly incident reminded us of how brutal and repressive our society still was. With the headlines screaming 'Queer Sort of Murder', the press had already given our lives yet another spin, leave alone the fact that there was little dignity for Pushkin or his family.

That a man had been killed did not matter, that he was gay and had porn in his room was what the press focused on. This was perhaps the first time I felt like speaking up for our community even though I was not yet openly gay at work. I called some senior journalists I knew in the mainstream papers, asking if I could write a piece under my alias.

While they welcomed the idea of an opinion article, my view was not welcome as it critiqued the press, its narrative and society. Written on 19 August 2004, my opening para was this: 'The speculative manner in which the bulk of the national media reported the murder of two men in New Delhi last week reveals more about its prejudices than about the case in question.' The reporting, I said, was so slanted that it gave an impression that Pushkin and Vishal (the person with him) would not have lost their lives had they been straight.

The story did not die down, as it became the flavour of that time, each publication trying to find an angle, making every report a scoop. With this approach, they were bound to miss the harassment many gay men went through at the hands of the police. Phones were taken away to access names and phone numbers. Random calls were made to many of my friends who had attended the party that Pushkin was at before he headed home with Vishal where he was murdered. Some of the people I knew were called to the police station for questioning, leaving us, frightened, not knowing what may happen next, who could be the target and if our sexual identities would be revealed.

We had been sullied yet again by the press and with Section 377 still in the form it was, we were running scared, going further underground and cancelling any party that had been scheduled at that time.

It was Rumy who called me a few days after Pushkin's murder. She had been working with him in a consultancy, a job she had taken after quitting the media. According to her account, Pushkin was not only sweet but also extremely quiet and reserved. He mingled little amongst the larger group, she told me

'After reading the news and the profiling of gay people, I now know why you would prefer to stay underground than risk humiliation and hate every day,' she said in a tense and slightly angry tone, upset with how the reports had panned out. At the end of that conversation, it was clear, she just wanted me to know she was around and that I had to be careful, fearing that I could be hurt one day.

Chapter Thirty-seven

IN NOVEMBER OF that year, I assumed the role of CEO at the PR firm. It was not something I sought out or had dreamt of, it just landed on my lap pushing me straight into the corporate world. I was an absolute novice at running a business and had very little knowledge about PR. I was fortunate to have a senior management resource looking after finance—that I still struggle to make sense of today—while the general running of the firm was left to me including client servicing, media relations and HR—the latter taking a fair bit of time in the initial months.

I was faced with multiple HR issues. Some had to do with anger problems and others with non-performance. The latter were always easier to deal with as performance was easier to access but conduct could be complex. We did have one employee who was known to be abusive, arrogant, violating every norm in the rulebook. He had spoken ill of some women, ran his own business from office and told his boss to leave the premises.

While he was ultimately asked to resign, following repeated recommendations from his team leader, it came to light that he had an immense dislike for me. His dislike emanated from his views on sexuality.

What I got to see after his departure was one of the many text messages (in English and Hindi) that he had sent out to employees at all levels, be it the doorman, executives, peon, trainees or team leaders. The messages claimed that I was a 'lesser man than he was and other men were'. He tried to provoke them to rise up against me 'a gay' as following my leadership was a sign of 'gutlessness'.

What he had done was out me and questioned my professional competence with an unrelated gauge of assessment, my sexual orientation. I was tormented by this incident although I never revealed any anxiety while reading the message, calling it 'creative writing'.

But that night the spiteful nature of the event left me feeling equally spiteful towards just about anyone in society and the city I lived in. Driving home, I had turned into the aggressive Delhi driver, pulling down my window, abusing all those who broke lanes and the law, which turned out to be almost everyone who was on my route.

I realized that being a CEO meant nothing, definitely not the security that leadership positions were assumed to give. 'Stop hyperventilating! Do your work and prove yourself through performance. Your rise in the professional world will save you,' Vinay told me when I called him that night. 'That's the system, you need to conform to it and work your way through.'

I took his advice and worked hard, really hard, but it wasn't a smooth run! A few months later a rumour did the rounds saying I was lesbian. While I laughed at the misrepresentation of facts, it did not stop there. Even the privacy of my laptop was invaded during a routine maintenance check, revealing some of the gay websites I had visited. There was talk that I was dating someone senior in the management—another single man.

By then I was numb, choosing to focus on what Vinay had said—working hard and being productive.

Chapter Thirty-eight

AFTER SEVERAL TRIPS to Thailand and many flings with young men from Manipur to Nagaland, I was most certainly a rice queen. No doubt the attraction was what it was, that is physical, but I was also absorbed by the simplicity and innocence that seemed to flow particularly in people from parts of the North East and in certain Southeast Asian cultures. There was a blend of urban and the old world, something that charmed and enamoured me.

Travelling to Thailand was not just about that. I think the anonymity that I had in a foreign country freed me from the trappings of Delhi and that of a CEO. Moreover, as one of my friends pointed out, even though I was open with Ma, I had unconsciously limited the frequency of visits by anyone, not knowing what would go through Ma's mind seeing different people visiting me from time to time.

Who knows, she would have to answer such questions from neighbours or even from our domestic help who had seen me grow up and had been with us for over two decades. This, as a consequence, made trips out of the city, particularly to Bangkok, opportunities to meet new men and forge relationships, turning hotel rooms and restaurants into private enough spaces for such explorations.

As it was, gay men preferred spaces of their own and privacy as the public glare left us with little room to breathe or to even stretch one's arms. Even today, if someone walked out of my room in the morning, even a close male friend who had stayed over, I would find the domestic help staring at him, probably itching with questions on who this person is and as usual, why had I not married. The paranoia was such that many friends I knew, as well as myself, felt we were being judged every second we stepped out into the open.

There were occasions I thought of moving out or taking a tiny room on rent to meet new friends and potential partners in the way gay men liked it, especially those who were new to my life. I even discussed this with my brothers. Duji said that it was a process of growing old and maturing and becoming independent. After all, he said, 'We live on our own, Pa had moved away from his family and even Ma was running a home even though we had all been a part of it'. Dilip agreed and said it was best to negotiate the situation and find a way out.

I pondered over the option. But I finally did not exercise it knowing I owed a lot to Ma for all that she had done for me. I also felt our lives were seamless in a special way, sharing the little and big things that occurred every day. I would never have peaceful sleep knowing Ma was alone, coming up from her clinic, eating dinner without me. I knew that I would miss her too. And, anyway, Delhi was already a hellish city for women of any age.

As the years went by burning the midnight oil, as they loved to say in the corporate world, I travelled to several parts of the world representing the firm and then even the industry as the president of Public Relations Consultancies Association of India (PRCAI). The travails opened my mind to the diversity of the world and a growing compassion for the LGBTQ community. The global network I was part of called the PROI (Public Relations Organisation International) was one such body that accepted and embraced everyone. I recall how a special reception was hosted at the home of a gay couple in one of the cities in the US.

While this made Delhi look even more horrible, the global

network encouraged me to be more myself than anyone else. As a consequence, I took Chala, my new Thai boyfriend, along with Ma to one of our global summits as it was a practice to travel with partners, spouses, children and parents, making it one large family.

Chala was one of those rare Thai men I had spent hours talking to before we decided to date. It was a strange beginning where our first interaction was hardly for a minute, exchanging cards at the Telephone Bar. Our second meeting was longer, over lunch where even Ma was present. She, of course, was unaware that we had never really met in the true sense of the word. He was relaxed, responding to questions from Ma, asking her about her visit to Bangkok and even about Delhi.

He was soon a part of our family. I invited him to Delhi more than once and he fitted in like our home was his home too, eating regular meals and cooking up some special Thai ones once in a while. The relationship got serious enough for us to consider living together in Delhi. We had mapped out ways to get a business visa, planning some language skill training programmes too, so that he could converse more easily in the retail industry that he had experience in.

As a family we had even decided that soon after he moved to Delhi, we would get engaged and throw a big party to celebrate the occasion. I recall Ma deciding not to sell a piece of gold jewellery so she could reuse it to make rings for us.

Our expectations, plans and dreams, however, came crashing as the sheer paperwork and requirements to live in India for Thais with his kind of qualification was nearly impossible. The laws, of course, were hindrances. Even if Thailand recognized same-sex marriages, which it didn't, India had Section 377. If both nations had a marriage law for homosexuals he could have been my spouse, reducing the hassles of immigration and removing the focus from qualifications or the need for a work visa.

There was little hope and as the months went by, the reality of things eroded what we had built, leaving us on separate paths.

I seemed to have hardened up as yet another chapter closed. I cried a little and privately. I had stopped speaking about Chala and did not encourage any conversation on the relationship that had ended. While Chala went on to find a local Thai around a year later, I fell off the gay map, sticking just to a handful of friends.

Chapter Thirty-nine

BY EARLY 2009, there were rumours and murmurs that there will finally be an order from the Delhi High Court on the Naz Foundation petition on Section 377. We were naturally hopeful but were not sure what to expect.

While the press was now more inclined towards us, if not neutral, there was the UPA government sending out mixed signals. Reports suggested that the Ministry of Home Affairs was opposed to striking down the law as homosexuality could not 'morally condoned', whereas the Ministry of Health and Family Welfare contended that Section 377 was 'counter-productive to the efforts of HIV/AIDS prevention and treatment'.

Some friends in the media said even the Congress party was split with the younger lot of leaders and a handful of seniors supporting the reading down of Section 377 whereas the others feared an electoral backlash. Religious groups, of course, invoked some god or the other, using morality of their own making, a measure to judge us, terming us mentally sick and criminals.

But on 2 July 2009, we finally got an order from the Delhi High Court decriminalizing consensual sex between men or 'gay sex', a term commonly used!

I was at the Moolchand Hospital with my mother, when the then resident editor of *Times of India*, Arindam Sengupta, called and said, 'Hey bugger, you are legit.' I had no idea what he was talking about so he clarified, 'Silly guy, the court has supported gay sex.' Arindam was one caring person. Just the previous year when Ma and I attended Pride together, he had connected with his bureau to ensure no photo of ours got published. He feared that Ma's social circle would not be kind. 'Even the corporate world may not have been very generous,' he had told me later.

I reached home early as instructed by Ma so that I could organize a small get-together that evening of friends including activists and lawyers. I knew almost no activists at that point other than Aditya Bandopadhyay, one of the lawyers. I called him, his then partner and a few other friends most of whom were designers and stylists. From a group of fifteen, we had over thirty at home, chomping on cake and snacking on wafers and nuts and of course drinking a bit before we headed out to a special night at PNP.

It was one of those unusual evenings where gay men had straight friends with them. Some of the heterosexuals, mostly young girls, were just out of college, hanging out with their set of gay men. It was not just about them being a fag hag but also about a certain kind of statement they wished to make that of being modern, liberated and breaking the norm.

I remember one such girl telling me at the spontaneous after-party held at my home that 'you should be happy this thing is gone'. I could not resist asking what she meant by 'this thing' and then asked about Section 377. 'I don't know about it but it is good it is gone, na?' she said, without even batting an eyelid.

She was like many others who cared little but fancied the 'coolness' of hanging out with people like us. I remember some of my friends saying that we were mere props or objects that didn't matter. If we did, they would have engaged with us to know us, how we lived and how harmful and ridiculous Section 377 had been and that their gay friends could be behind bars for having sex with another man!

As much as we wanted to dismiss a girl like her, more because of our angst with society at large, we knew having her on our side mattered at that juncture. It was about safety in numbers for many young men.

The order by Justice A. P. Shah and Justice S. Muralidhar, was not merely historic, it said something that touched us all: 'Section 377 denies a gay person a right to full personhood which is implicit in notion of life under Article 21' of the Constitution. At that point many commercial establishments such as bars and cafes opened up in Delhi providing more options than a PNP or a spot on a rooftop bar in CP. I remember an advertisement in a daily lifestyle supplement of a large liquor brand using the rainbow colours for a party to celebrate diversity. Even a 'Bird Cage' party was held somewhere.

Even I opened up. That August, Bharat I. Sharma was finally vanquished as I wrote about the new pink economy in the *Hindustan Times* with one of my colleagues. In an article titled 'In the Pink of Wealth' we wrote about Mirage, a pub in the Crowne Plaza Hotel, nightclubs such as Elevate, 24X7 at The Lalit, Tamang Gang at the DLF Promenade and Liquid Kitchen that all had at least one gay night. And the money that could be made on a single night was at least ₹2 lakh, Manish Sharma of Boyzone told us.

The party scene aside, there were parlours such as NYC catering to men only; it was for those of us who felt embarrassed getting waxed or threaded. There was also a more visible gay travel agency— InjaPink that organized holidays for the community.

'This was bound to happen, Sharif,' one of my friends told me one evening over drinks. 'No one remembers what happened in Lucknow and the reason for this case and why we needed Section 377 read down.'

It was in 2001 that the police in Lucknow raided parks as well as the offices of an NGO and picked up male and transgender sex workers, their customers, innocent gay men and other health workers, one by one, alleging a sex racket. Local newspapers to national dailies had characterized our community in the most one-sided way, alleging that those working in the area of AIDS/HIV were essentially people who thrived on prostitution or were a cover for such a 'business'.

This was the time when Arif Jafar, the man who set up one of the first gay groups in India was tortured. With him, several others lay in jail for over forty days, being denied bail. The then magistrate reportedly called homosexuality a 'curse on society' and sections of the Fourth Estate said homosexuality was a Western import. At that time it was more about prejudices than Section 377 itself as anti-sodomy and anti-obscenity laws were used against those who were arrested.

Aditya was amongst the lawyers who first rushed to Lucknow to deal with the case in the lower court. Following him were seniors such as Indira Jaisingh and Anand Grover taking up the matter in the high court. There were very few people speaking up in Lucknow with the exception of Saleem. It was finally voices from Delhi, then Bengaluru and Mumbai that rose to fight the matter.

Those were the days that our human rights and such acts of mental and physical torture did not matter at all. I recall Anjali once telling me how she had to fight to save a boy who was undergoing shock therapy at a prestigious hospital in South Delhi to convert him 'back' to heterosexuality.

Sadly, such 'therapy' continues even now by 'trusted' doctors. I had friends being taken to such clinics by their parents, adding to their mental trauma, leading to a further erosion of confidence. Some of them had priests coming home conducting all kinds of prayers and others went through a different kind of hell taking hormone-based pills with shock therapy. I was fortunate that Ma had not pursued such a path with me, nor did my extended family!

The situation in Lucknow had us in Delhi very worried. As a community, we had to steal every nook and corner to make it ours. Dark alleys in Connaught Place, the dimly lit toilets in the lanes between the various blocks in the inner circle and the Central

Park which now has the main hub of the metro rail network, were places to cruise and find men.

If someone had the guts, a quick tug into one of the filthy toilets in the market for a quick kiss, hug, letting hands run over each other's bodies, was not uncommon. If you were in the South, you could explore your 'gayness' by picking up someone on the streets of South Extension market or outside a prime hotel in RK Puram—these were the areas where even straight men found women. Only a few could afford to pay an entry to private parties, pool-ins or PNP.

As a group who had come out much earlier, we did not see this disparity changing easily, particularly in the classist society of Delhi. Some would leverage the 'pink' money and the power equations that capital played and others would be left out. This meant that those who sought the dark areas of any big city would continue to do so as the order could never have guaranteed a change in how society viewed us. Why else was anonymity on gay chat sites growing even after 2009 and till today?

We all agreed that the order was a historic one for obvious reasons and particularly beneficial for the new generation which was teeming with energy and a libido that was jumping with excitement.

Now they had the freshness of freedom and we the experience of time and a censored life.

Chapter Forty

EVEN AS THE lay of the land started to change mildly and slightly for the LGBTQ community after the court order, my trips to South East Asia did not reduce. Duji had noticed this, terming me the 'wandering' man, 'running away from Delhi' at the drop of a hat.

He made these remarks over a phone call, going on to ask what had made things tick with Chala. 'He fitted into the family, Ma liked him, he seemed to just stroll in,' I replied saying it would have been easy to settle down with him had things worked legally. 'Really?' Duji asked. 'It was about fitting into the structure at home and with Ma?' he asked. 'Are you looking at a similar set-up for your whole life?' he continued.

He explained what he meant, 'When you love someone, you need to love that person and not ensure if others do or not, even if it is Ma. It is for you to live with that person, not Ma or any aunt or uncle or friend. Your relationship and love doesn't need any endorsement. It needs for the two of you to be in it. I just see you trying to be like others, not who you are in actuality!'

'Believe me, everyone who matters to you will bless you for the choice you make, even Ma,' he told me. 'Live your life, find your space, say and do what you wish, love who you want.'

However, I had lost confidence in dating and was disinterested in the party scene, often yawning out of boredom or exhaustion from work. It wasn't unusual for me to be up till 2 a.m. working away, writing emails and making plans for the next day, week or even months.

I remember crying as our family put together a collection of articles of my father, reading his views and making sense of the world of his time. He never minced his words. He never held back. Maybe just reading what Pa had to say at his time touched some chord within me. Perhaps Duji was right that I had curtailed my own freedom of expression, not saying or doing what I wanted.

I had started to cry very often, sometimes under the shower, in my room, listening to a song or even as I spoke to my team on the journey of the firm and its success at that point. At the back of my mind, I think, was a growing consciousness that something had to change, even if it were my line of work or life in general.

I longed for someone, I craved to be in bed, hugging and holding on to a person who would say 'I know', a person who would take care of me, a peaceful romance, a beautiful space, a garden in front, cooking together, early morning coffees and teas, music and everything that defined calmness. I wanted to come home to someone, even if I had to wait for him to return from his workplace.

I was obviously toying with different ideas of freedom, none of which had seemed real so far. I had deleted gay chat apps and kind of created a shell to survive in only allowing myself an occasional massage, which was also more for therapy than a happy ending. In any case, it was not fulfilling. I had also tried retail therapy, shopping pointlessly, buying watches and shoes, but I was more often than not saddened after each purchase instead of being happier.

As I sank into these moods, I realized that it had been more than three years since Chala and I had parted ways. I could not even remember when was the last time I saw someone as a potential boyfriend. Even if there was such a man and I had met him, I was too sluggish to give that person a thought. I was so damn tired.

Chapter Forty-one

However morose things were, I found a ray of happiness with the return of Adi to India. He had been away in San Francisco for around six years returning on my forty-third birthday. He literally flew in and came home for the small party I had organized, his flame burning bright as ever.

He was going to join the firm I was heading. He had worked there long before my entry into the firm. Over a call before heading back, he had warned me that he was not used to concealing his sexuality. I wondered how he would adjust to an Indian office or how others would respond to him.

Adi's arrival was an in-your-face display of queerness. He would walk about the office showing off his 'happy socks', talked about the new drapes in his house, and once even discussed what it was like to wear stockings with one of our young consultants. He spoke with ease about his life, about the potential dates and sometimes even shared photos of men who were pinging him on a gay chat site. For some, initially, he was a disruption but soon they got used to him when they realized that he was absolutely harmless.

What his presence did was allow for more conversations on LGBTQ, easing the confinement that some other gay men at work may have felt. In fact, some women colleagues opened up saying they were curious and considering exploring their sexuality. As a result, by then even a brainstorming session for a consumer brand had a queer angle.

In time, my singlehood became a matter of concern for some of my colleagues who tried to set me up with men they thought were gay, sending me photos over the phone. The photos included one of a trainee—Prateek—who was working with one of our clients. He was young, slim, had brownish eyes, brown skin and a warm smile that at times revealed shyness.

I met him at an office function. I commented only on his stylish shoes to start a conversation. Soon, I realized that he was dating a woman, so it was pointless doing much more than looking at him. However, we did not lose touch and occasionally indulged in serious to silly conversations where I finally made it evident that I liked him.

We exchanged messages over Facebook, Instagram and WhatsApp, pretty much following each other's lives. He did not mind our conversations layered with sexual innuendos—something that often happened when he was drunk and 'speaking the truth' as he claimed.

One evening though, a couple of whiskeys down, he insisted on meeting me, coming over home, to share something very personal. The conversation was unexpected. He first asked what it was like to be gay, did I ever feel attracted to a woman, had I slept with one and what were gay relationships like. I shared my experience but questioned him, 'Why do you ask?'

Prateek had wanted to 'try out' what it was like to sleep with a man. 'I think that curiosity has come and gone but not gone fully,' he told me. And he was just eight months away from his wedding then!

'Why don't we make out?' he asked very suddenly.

At first I refused, reminding him of his impending wedding and that we were just friends and typically friends don't make out. 'Friends with benefits?' he interjected, suggesting we forget about the wedding that evening. 'You are a nice guy and you've always liked me,' he pointed out, turning off his phone after telling his fiancée that he was busy in a meeting, simultaneously stripping down to his underwear.

It was one of the most delightful experiences of my life, the element of surprise that someone as beautiful as Prateek who I thought was straight was ready to go almost all the way and down on me. There was an instant chemistry between us. His happy eyes, the kiss, it all seemed so special! His slim frame in my arms, the laughter, his desire to please me, were memorable. No doubt the long drought of intimacy may have added to the pleasure but that it was Prateek and not any other random person was what distinguished him and that time from the rest.

Prateek, of course, was gone. His wedding took place as planned and his conversations with me became occasional courtesies that meant nothing any more.

'Aren't men like this, undecided, bisexual, opportunists?' the colleague who introduced me to him said, visibly upset with what had happened. I shrugged my shoulders. 'I don't know, but he was so good, so beautiful!' I wouldn't mind having him back if he ever got divorced.

The marriage, however, seems to be intact—from what one can see. He remains connected though over WhatsApp, as very recently, when he came to watch me on stage, he messaged: 'My eyes will be on you!'

Chapter Forty-two

THINGS WERE EVOLVING around us there was greater queer-focused reportage in the media, subtle to harsh depictions in cinema and conversations at work. I felt it was the right time to re-look at our HR policies, making them more conducive for women, live-in relationships and LGBTQ. The way to bring this change, I thought, was through discussion and debates. As a result, the Friday Open House became more engaging and emotionally charged at times, covering topics such as women's depiction in the media, politics, religion, black money, corruption, gay rights and Indian history.

The series of discussions opened minds, allowed us to collectively engage with diverse thoughts and also helped us learn to understand each other better as people. In a way, the work culture became a lot more humane, encouraging a positive evolution in policy.

Even the way we assessed performance and increments was approached differently, with a growing weightage given to the lowest and middle levels. I saw the workplace as a pyramid where the bottom required the greatest attention and handholding as the top already had access to a far better life, knowledge, experience and the privilege of power to bring change.

In a way, my views of the outside world where the wealth gap was increasing and irresponsibility growing at the top, reflected in the way I wanted to run the firm. Much earlier I had initiated the process to reduce the dominance of Delhi—the headquarters—be it in strategy or leadership, so that the idea of the nation is not determined by a single city and mindset, ensuring we have a mixed flavour in all we do.

At all points, I guess I was unconsciously challenging the typical power structures and systems, something I deeply believed was so wrong, as it had wronged me and my community too. I remember a friend in the industry telling me that what I was trying was unique and challenging and probably even a form of my own activism. 'It was a subtle attack on capitalism,' he had said.

Simultaneously, my workplace and colleagues (who were now becoming friends), was my only world. We were socializing so often that I left myself with no space for anyone beyond them. I also denied myself time to engage with my heart and soul, maybe intentionally feeling more secure at work than with my emotions.

Still, even if there were many lovely evenings of songs, dances and conversations, I also had many tearful hours, writing poems that embraced my sadness and expressed my depression, a word I didn't use then.

If I ever went on a date—once in a quarter of a year or so—I would be bored or scared that someone might show interest. I think I feared committing to a person or relationship and hence had stopped responding to any person who wished to see me more than once. In contrast, if the man or boy was gorgeous but emotionally vulnerable—the kind that I was years ago, falling in love with intimacy—I would close the door on him too, refusing the much-needed sexual release.

What I was left with was music—karaoke nights at a bar in Ansal Plaza. This became a ritual for every Friday night. At first, it was just with friends from office but it slowly expanded to encompass a growing set of new people at the bar. This place was a great find as there were musically aware karaoke jockeys (KJs), who were also gay friendly much like Big Chill and Defence Bakery.

It was then, midway through a night, when the idea of forming a band took birth. I remember saying, 'Before I turn fifty, I want to perform on stage and act in a play or a film!' I asked the folks around me that night if they wished to be a part of this, singing with a live band and they all said yes.

The band was given the name Friends of Linger. Linger came from the word 'ling', which meant gender and gender inclusive. The 'er' was added only to fend off any criticism, hate or anger from religious fundamentalists. I turned to a local session artist I knew of—Adhir Ghosh—the son of family friends, Ena and Arup. He instantly put together a team of musicians called the Classic Collective to back us up. We also decided to turn some of my poetry into song. The poetry included comments on economics, public policy, capitalism, love, rape and on being gay.

Our first single was 'Head Held High', reportedly the only track dedicated to the LGBTQ community at that time. It was to be the feature of our first gig scheduled for 19 December 2013 at Delhi's Hard Rock Cafe. Composed by Smiti Malik and Adhir, the song was meant to be celebratory in nature. The lyrics of the song referred to the various stages of not knowing, curiosity, certainty, and then to stand up for one's right, not feeling ashamed of who one was.

But what we did not know then was that soon it would be a song of protest too—a consequence of the Supreme Court order that had come six days earlier, reversing the Delhi High Court order of 2009.

I remember I was sitting in office, reading the news flash, with tears rolling down my eyes. I banged my fist on the table in anger, anxiously pulling my hair back, looking out of the window as I moved restlessly in the swivel chair. I called Ma complaining about the courts, the culture and society. 'What a life to lead in this shitty country!' I said. Ma didn't get a chance to say much as I kept the call brief wanting to call others but she did manage to say, 'I can't believe the courts would do this.'

I reached out to friends and lawyers and then the media, just trying to make sense of what had happened as well as to share my angst. This was the first time one could see some sort of unity against the Apex Court's decision with strong views coming even from political circles, friends and family and the press.

Thanks to organizations such as the Delhi Queer Pride and other activists, we all got together in protest, anger, love and unity. I cannot forget how Gautam Bhan stood up on a makeshift platform in the Jantar Mantar area speaking in English and Hindi with a kind of passion that was not often seen. This is pretty much when the slogan 'No Going Back' on Section 377 was coined. From Facebook profile pictures to cover photos, to wall posts, this slogan appeared everywhere even at Pride.

Of course, this ghastly order, took our preparations a little off guard, derailing a few sessions of practice as well. But on 19 December, we took stage with some ten artists—nine of whom had become allies—belting out a variety of songs and singing 'Head Held High' for the first time. And in the audience were Ma and Duji who was visiting Delhi, proudly waving the rainbow flag as we sang this song.

As *HT City*'s local edition did a near full page on the song that very day, we had an audience of over two hundred people supporting the band, 'Head Held High' and our fundamental rights. I remember my first sign of public anger was putting out my views on the order as well as how a certain 'yoga guru' was so wrong in assuming he could cure us. I remember the cheers that night as well as collectively booing that the SC order and the heads of religious groups received.

This, I guess, was my first step into the arena of activism, through the soft and subtle means of music.

Chapter Forty-three

AS MUCH AS we blamed the British Raj for Section 377, who could deny our ability to forget history, our scriptures and realize how unfair and warped our thinking was. I recall discussing these matters with several friends knowing full well it would make little difference other than allow me some time to vent my frustration.

Every effort that followed the Apex Court order, as we were moving into 2014, such as the curative petition or the outcry in the media, was positive in intent although we knew that we were at the lower end of a steep road.

My desire to speak up, at that point in time though, was strange considering how the order of 2009 had not made much of a difference to my life. I guess my fears had reduced over the years as I kept coming out to more and more people I remember when *HT City* did that large report on our song, Ma had said, 'Now everyone knows about you.' I had replied, 'Only those who had read that article would know.' Probably that news report changed things or the presence of Ma and Duji waving the Pride flag at my band's first gig.

Even as I seemed to rise as a person, we were hit with the worst possible news, that Duji had cancer. Ma had virtually moved to London to look after him, staying at Uma masi's home. I also made several visits to spend time with him and Ma. He and I got closer than ever before, discussing life, existence and purpose.

One morning in London, not having to respond to phone calls or emails, it struck me that there was a lot more to life than work and balance sheets. The peace of the morning, the space for the mind and the conversations with Duji about his health were all converging somewhere in my head. I had never chased money or earned a huge salary (as compared to what my market value was said to be), but that is all that I had done for close to a decade now.

It was then that I wrote about long distance relationships, globalization and how 'there is no space for love, as it's just a big business'. I wrote another poem on the lies we tell, be it at work or at home or in matters of love.

I had tears in my eyes watching couples walk in the parks in London or beside the Thames. I saw a vibrant gay life on the streets of Soho and even that saddened me. I wept thinking of Duji and all the love he gave to many of his friends and the strangers he met. I remember how he guided me, and what his idea of protection was—liberation to test the waters and the limits that one could go to, not a manual of risk averseness or overt caution. 'To accept is to engage. To tolerate is to ignore the truth,'—this is a line he and I had coined.

It was he who told me that it was high time I used my communication skills for a better purpose, if it would make me happier. He knew full well I was in depression and the way to come out of it was not just seeking help but picking a path that suited my mind and the person I had to be—a gay man without apology and no fear.

I pretty much picked up the pen, filled it with a huge quantity of ink—in a manner of speaking—and started writing on topics I had not yet addressed. There was a desire to write, to speak and be heard. I was never, nor am I now, an expert or an intellectual on sexuality or religion or even human rights. My own life was a learning in itself, and I just tried to apply logic and common sense, in the way I knew it. I wrote about patriarchy not just imposing itself on women but also how it disallowed men to be anyone else other than the alpha male. I also wrote about the toxic masculinity that was prevalent in our society. I wrote how Section 377 was ruining innocent lives and marriages and why homophobia not homosexuality was a mental health problem. I also wrote what it was to grow old being gay.

I might have written dozens of articles over the next 12–15 months as my mind kept ticking and Duji continued to inspire me, filling my inbox with write-ups from across the world on the LGBTQ movement and crimes against us. I shared with him some of our upcoming songs on identity, sexuality and diversity. He, of course, was always encouraging, waiting to hear the final product.

Over the next ten weeks or so, Duji and I spent a lot of time together as he moved to Delhi, returning to India after twenty-five years. It never seemed he would be going any time soon given the alertness of his mind, his positivity and how he shared information, chatted about my future or listened to music. But, on 30 October 2015, he was gone.

He was one of the few people who knew me well, maybe better than I knew myself. It was the hardest time for our family, especially for Ma in particular whose strength had taken a beating. I could hear her cry in the early mornings, around 4-4.30 a.m., not knowing whether I should hold her or allow her that space to grieve.

I cried too but often held back, as one of us at home had to be stable; also, I had an office to go to. It was only in the month of April, six months later, that the facade collapsed when I was sitting alone in my room in an empty home. I had just returned from the UK and had left Ma with Uma masi after attending an event in honour of Duji hosted by Warwick University.

The emotional fatigue, helplessness and continued depression, took their toll. I called Sonu and Dilip several times and started crying as soon as they took the call. I was feeling not only helpless and alone but also lonely. For the first time, Dilip shouted at me saying it was about time I found a partner, that I had undermined the value of love and companionship. They both felt I should consider relocating to a more conducive environment than carry on in Delhi. 'As you grow older, it becomes even tougher to foster a relationship, whether you are gay or not,' Sonu said.

I was soon diagnosed with burnout and deep depression as my knees weakened and ears rang. The doctors said that I should shut shop immediately, close my home and go to the hills or to a beach or to any peaceful place I would like to be in. I went to Dilip and Sonu's home, unsure of my ability to be alone. The calm of their home, the peace in the area and the silence of their backyard did work as a balm but it was far from enough.

Even as I contemplated resigning from work and staying away from Delhi, I returned again to music as a healer. I pulled out an old poem:

> I miss you when I am smiling
> I miss you when it's grey
> I miss you when I'm lying
> Trying to sleep in my bed
> I miss you in the morning
> I miss you through the day
> I miss you when it's sunny
> And when sunlight turns away
> So if I call you, will you be awake
> Will you tell me, you forgive my mistakes
> So I remind you, I'm not heaven sent
> Will you tell me, not all is lost and our love can stay

This poem turned into a same-sex ballad titled 'Miss You' writ with regret of having given in to marriage with a woman, rather than continuing with a boyfriend whom I missed deeply. Some journalists who interviewed me assumed that this song was written for a special person, not knowing that I was missing a partner, not anyone. At times while performing it on stage, I had to choke back my tears because the longing was so strong.

As it happened, the song got recognized as a part of the LGBTQ movement in an article by *Youth Ki Awaaz* that covered the history of the movement and its milestones. What got noticed was our victory over the CBFC's decision to cut ten seconds of the video, which we appealed against and won finally in the Appellate Tribunal on 25 January 2017. The footage in question was a scene of separation with two men initially lying in bed and one getting up to leave in anger. There was nothing sexual or vulgar—not even a kiss or hug in those ten seconds.

My ultimate purpose in fighting the case was to reclaim a space of entertainment and storytelling that I believed was ours too and not just for mainstream ideas and narratives of life and love. After all, the music video was already live on the then relatively freer digital and social spaces of YouTube and Facebook, collectively having over 50,000 views at the time we won the case.

In my plea, I addressed the areas of education and awareness and accused the board of homophobia—something that then CBFC chief denied in a news report. This is what I said about the video: 'It revolves around love and a relevant social issue that has led to spoiling dozens of marriages and victimizing innocent men and women. This video, in fact, is educative in nature and might bring some awareness amongst many who would watch this if it were allowed to be shown on television.'

I further claimed, 'in comparison with a lot of approved "Universal" content on TV related to women, gender, violence, love and marriage,' it appears that the approach of the CBFC is different and 'the board has appeared homophobic or does not understand the narrative or the context'.

The presentation to the tribunal, which included film actor, Poonam Dhillon and journalist Shekhar Iyer, was calm and peaceful with almost no questions. Ms Dhillon, in fact, came up to me, held my hand, smiled and shook her head, probably saying she knew what I felt. Whatever she may have meant, I was beaming with joy.

I recall looking up at the sky soon after exiting the meeting with the Tribunal talking to Duji, telling him we had won. I called Ma, Chitra, Venu and Adi, sharing the news, realizing that we had to fight, and only then could we win.

Chapter Forty-four

THE WIN OVER the CBFC was a temporary relief, emotionally and mentally. The passage out of depression was to be a longer one, leading me to question my competence as a professional and my ability to love and be loved. Even to take stage again became a task and not a pleasurable activity.

One of my doctors prescribed sleeping pills and medication to soothe my anxious nerves. I feared addiction, a lifelong one, of the drugs, much like some of the patients I heard about from friends in the US.

I even went to shrinks. One of them seemed uncomfortable with my sexuality and the other was indecisive and inconclusive, giving me no direction other than weekly bills that I had to pay, asking me to visit her again and again. I turned to Sonu, making calls past midnight and then to some of my dear ones—Mehtab, Bijoya and Minal—who listened patiently, knowing they were too far away to sit with me, hold my hand and guide me out of my mess.

I was, of course, on my own now.

This is when I decided to clear the clutter I had created over the years. I isolated one thing after another. First, I closed the doors on any past flings or persons I had fancied, blocking them on social networks and my phone. I had never done that probably hoping someone would return. Then, I deleted all gay chat apps, again, as I had found them tiresome, having pretty much the same kind of conversations that I used to have years ago. I had come to the conclusion—right or wrong—that these were largely distractions and show windows rather than a space to find substance to build something on. I guess I was searching for common ground and 'real' interactions, the tangible intagibles of an equation between two people, taking seed in an open space rather than on a smartphone.

I started to discard and give away the many shoes I had, leaving myself with fewer pairs. I also handed out some of the watches I had accumulated over the years. Even extra, unworn clothes were emptied out of my cupboard. I vowed not to buy anything for myself if it weren't of utility on a day-to-day basis or evergreen in nature and neutral in colour.

I also reduced my hours at the PR firm and worked for most part from home, being more of a mentor and consultant, making my visits to the office less frequent for a few months. The four walls of my room at home, turned into a divine space transiting from a think-pad to creative space to workplace, depending on my mind, its thoughts and the compulsions of work.

All of this helped me break the monotonous pattern of my life, gradually developing a purpose of sorts which remained undefined at that point. I realized that sharing and talking was one way to move out of where I was. Consequently, speaking, poetry and prose (that I had attempted earlier in a different frame of mind) became cathartic and the new spaces I explored through forums and groups helped me learn a lot more about others, queer life, challenges, privileges I had and the ways others were traversing the minefields of daily life.

It was at a Gaylaxy event themed 'Breaking the Closet' that I met Anwesh Sahoo who told me of his journey, coming from a small town and not being accepted by his family. While he won the Mr Gay India pageant in 2016, a pageant hosted and owned by the Big Boss star, drag artist, singer and model, Sushant Divgikar, he went through the normative views of colour, facing racism from within the community, not being seen as a beauty that should represent India on the global stage. 'The evils of the heterosexual world existed in us as well,' he told me.

I also met Gautam Yadav, who surprised me with his normalization of HIV, living with it as though it was diabetes. He belonged to a family that lived in a home that was slightly better than a slum. His father had accepted his sexuality and HIV, caring for him for who he was. He was now one of the best counsellors on the subject, representing the nation at international conferences, living a life he might not have imagined. His concern was the lack of information on the disease, the recklessness amongst men having sex with men and fear amongst the gay community to get tested. 'We need more people working in this area; men were taking too many risks,' he said.

There was also Sukhdeep Singh who had come out through a blog in 2009, going on to set up *Gaylaxy* magazine, creating a space for many a queer person. His challenges, when I met him, were less about being gay and more about sustaining the online gay space of expression he had created. 'It is difficult to pay bills, retain a job and keep the platform alive,' he said expressing a concern that was not going away any time soon.

Often I felt incomplete and a misfit in the admirable presence of the many new faces and voices pushing the LGBTQ case forward. 'Do what you can now,' my dear friend and colleague Sujay Mehdudia told me once, suggesting there was never a right time for anything, certainly not for a movement such as ours. This was a perfect thing to say to me at a time when I was searching for a purpose. What was strange though that Sujay had never been exposed to anything queer and he was unsure about what the homosexual world was and how human we were. 'I am learning from you,' he would tell me so many times, admitting he may have carried some biases had we not met.

I was soon speaking and sharing platforms with the new lot, attending a queer march organized by a students' wing of IIT-

Delhi. I joined the accomplished queer slam poet Divya Dureja and vibrant transgender activist Abhina Aher at an event held by an NGO, sharing the diversity of our lives. I also addressed the media at a workshop organized by the Canadian High Commission, reminding them of their responsibility to broaden the narrative and depiction of people like us.

Soon, even my local club in Gulmohar Park agreed to open its space for a Gaylaxy Queer Carnival and a Harmless Hugs curtain-raiser for the international film and theatre festival. I dug in and associated myself with the global initiative—Open for Business—and started building an economic case for LGBTQ inclusion at the workplace. I began to absorb how the world could change if those with access to a system could use it for our greater benefit.

Those with limited resources, though, were chugging along as well. It wasn't only about private and public queer groups on Facebook, it was also about the emergence of informal organisations such as QKnit and Queer Kala in Mumbai, both run by a young activist named Sumit Pawar. It wasn't unusual for him to be seen at just about every Pride march in the country, reporting live, allowing people at a distance a glimpse of what was happening on ground.

Similarly, there were bike rides with 'allies' actively supporting events organized by young professionals and activists such as Harsh Agarwal in Delhi. There were trans-men to trans-women, walking shoulder to shoulder in some groups, sharing stories and experiences, good and bad. Lesbians were more visible too. There were drag artists coming from Kerala to Assam to Odhisha to Uttar Pradesh, touring the country with the support of commercial establishments such as nightclubs—Kitty Su for example—which had established a gay night every Thursday which was organized by a member of the Delhi Queer Pride group, Mohnish Malhotra.

What was common though was that just about every new leader and voice was under thirty if not just over twenty, pushing their way through and not hesitating to say what they wished, wearing their queerness with pride!

None of this existed during my early days, nor had I heard of people being aware of their sexuality as early as thirteen years of age. 'I can't imagine how you lived in the dark for almost three decades,' Anwesh exclaimed.

As satiating as these changes in queer life were, not everyone had the same share of the pie. I recall my friend, the drag artist Lush (Ayushman Aishwarya), telling me how his 'effeminate' body language denied him roles in Delhi's theatre circuit, a space that should have been liberal. Even Ikshaku Bezbaroa, who went by the drag name Kusbhoo, saw his six-year relationship come to an end, as his boyfriend was uncomfortable with his drag avatar, fearing the public glare.

While many of the younger lot were comfortable with themselves—single or in relationships—finding love easily in colleges or in the growing queer spaces in universities and NGOs, there were many still struggling with unacceptability at home and the lack of a family to turn to. The fear of being outed was also prevalent with words such as discreet being commonly used on chat sites, some even refusing to meet or being seen with anyone camp or effeminate. 'Straight-acting' as a description for a person's behaviour and mannerisms, that we grew up with, had not yet gone away.

Even the normative in the workplace was problematic as most organizations looked at inclusion as a 'cause' for women. Alex Mathew, aka Maya, the Drag Queen, had struggled to keep a job in corporate India, as his queerness was not acceptable. Another young activist, Bhuwan Kathuria, had once told me that he was out at work but many of his gay colleagues remained closeted at work and at home. 'I have a supportive family and that helps as nothing else matters,' he said, adding that even a positive ecosystem at work was not always the solution.

It was only a few leaders such as Parmesh Shahani who

headed Godrej's Culture Lab, who adopted diversity and inclusion as a culture, going beyond LGBTQ, into other divides and marginalization. It was at one such closed-door discussion that we first met, exchanging ideas, as well as being amused by a corporate head of a large MNC who revealed his sense of inclusion defined by his hoisting the rainbow flag on Pride day. Tokenism, as we both knew, was hardly a solution or a show of intent. 'It was like hoisting the Indian flag and claiming that you are doing something for the nation!' I had told a gathering.

However idealistic it may sound, the larger solution lay in a comfortable home, workplace and the journey between the two—a privilege that I now had—even if I had lost years in a period of history that was hardly remarkable. 'The authentic self is an essential,' Apurva Asrani, the award-winning scriptwriter and editor from Bollywood, had told me on the sidelines of a workshop, connecting freedom of the self with life, livelihood and economics. We both agreed that 'unfortunately' success had become an antidote to discrimination against our community, whereas our rights ideally should have been naturally ours at birth.

Apurva was embraced by his parents when he went on to win a Filmfare Award for his editing skills for the film *Satya*, resulting in his home being flooded with flowers and neighbours seeking his autograph. A lawyer friend of mine was accepted by his family when he joined one of the largest legal firms, going on to speak at international forums. Similarly, another friend got his due when he was interviewed in a leading pink daily as a leader of the future.

There were many such stories, I realized. And, I wondered how good this was for an actual movement going forward as success itself, as defined, was an imposed 'dream', articulated by the mainstream, a normative in itself. In short, what was being embraced was the final product of a commercial system rather than the person and what it is to be gay; what was needed was acceptance in a truer sense.

However, as some of us discussed this often, we took on board the reality of life and that many who were secure in the system were slowly emerging as advocates for our rights. What, of course, was of concern was whether those privileged through the system, including me, were equipped enough to speak for all.

Chapter Forty-five

AS I GOT drawn into the area of activism, I finally quit my full-time job, putting the lid on a decade-long tenure in public relations, absolutely unsure of what lay ahead. There was a sense of liberty, space, privacy and no routine as such which at times troubled me since I was accustomed to having a plan for a day, week, month or even a year for most of my life.

This new 'routine' though or the lack of, was perhaps the second coming of freedom after I called off my engagement with Samrita.

I had precious little work on my plate other than some writing assignments and a few hours of consultancy for the Safe Masti campaign on HIV awareness, giving me most of my days and nights to myself, away from emails and phone calls. I was now less structured and more instinctive, writing new songs, meeting more activists and building a platform with my friend, Pankaj Malhotra who ran an event firm—Epic—and Sujay, to blend music and arts with issues of social justice.

I also rediscovered the private party space, going to several of them quite often in search of someone that could stimulate my mind and heart. I also made random phone calls hoping to go out on a date, just to rekindle the sense of longing or even belonging to someone, or even for a few hours of intimacy.

This is when Christopher resurfaced in my life.

He was someone I had met probably once or twice a year over the last five years. He was also amongst the few people who had visited me when I was laid up in bed with a meniscus tear a couple of years ago. He had brought me a bouquet of flowers and expressed his care through his tender eyes and gentle hand that caressed my cheeks on that day, wishing me a quick recovery.

Straight out of Manipur, he had always been interested in me but I had never responded the same way, unable to find anything in common beyond the physicality of each other. The fact though was I had never tried hard enough to know him better, either due to depression and fears of failing yet again in a relationship or because of the constant reminder from family and friends to find someone equal, whatever that meant.

But now, there was something new about him. There was wit, he was chatty and sounded far more confident than the meek, silent person I had known. Christopher literally stormed into my life, bringing in a kind of joy I had never had. I recall laughing so much that I had fallen off the bed, with my stomach aching. He stayed over very often and his shyness had gone away as he built a rapport with Ma. They spent time together, doing what they both liked—gardening.

He was one of those few people who gave me so much peace that I could sleep off with my head on his shoulder. He was staying back at our home so regularly that soon he had some cupboard space for his clothes, and the guitar that he loved to strum had found a corner in the room as though it belonged there. I admired his ability to play along, sing and even make attempts to create our own tracks. These were the dimensions of him that I had been oblivious of until now.

Christopher reminded me what it meant to be cared for, what it was to be loved and how lovely it would be if one had a companion who shared similar values. Over the months, it became clear that our sexual escapades of the past were just that—sexual intimacy, a need of the time—but now it was truly lovemaking where there was so much fun, affection and comforting familiarity.

We had become so open with each other that we stripped down our past and placed it before ourselves, not that we even needed to. He had had two long distance relationships, one after the other, neither of which had matured into a strong bond thus allowing him the occasional dates with others and myself. One was with a man from Uttar Pradesh who was already married and the other was with a German who worked with a foreign airline, Delhi being an occasional stop where Christopher kept him company.

Such long distance relationships were not uncommon where the foreigner was showcased as a friend and a tourist and not a lover or a partner. It gave people like Christopher who were closeted the freedom to have the 'foreigner' over for a few days or to travel with him on short vacations, without being questioned. Our relationship, however, was distinctively different—we were both in the same city and our time together was not seasonal.

The relationship was peaking just around my forty-ninth birthday which came soon after a three-week vacation in Bangkok, Hua Hin and Pattaya. We had described this trip as a honeymoon. And Ma told Christopher that she had never seen me as happy as I was in a long time and all the 'credit' went to him.

While we spent a lot of time at home, I had started visiting him too. To me, these were the most special moments, being served by him—the master of the house. I felt so comfortable in his small and clean apartment that I did not feel like getting up from there. There was peace and a sense of ownership that I still cannot put into a sentence. Maybe it was the feeling that this was 'our' space, even though it wasn't.

However, the fact that Christopher and I were so close had become a problem he had not told me about and probably had not even foreseen.

In the ghetto-like life of his and the scheduled tribe he belonged to, with friends and relatives from his village living in the same vicinity, word had got around about 'this friend' of his with whom he spent a lot of time—me. The fact that he had not been out on a date or shown interest in girls had raised the antenna amongst some. If any of this talk were to reach his parents, they would be tormented and abused and he would be denied entry into his village and home—something he could never imagine.

While Christopher had lifted my spirits, the end of our relationship sent me crashing into bouts of tears, and sleeplessness. Every other conversation with a friend would be about him and why this had happened to us, ending with a hope that we would find a way out. I can't remember wanting or needing someone so much as Christopher. It took months for us to come to a complete closure with him picking up his clothes and guitar—things that now seemed so much part of the room.

I found the end hard to believe. Everything had been perfect. He cried a lot sitting in my car as I saw him off. I cried too. I recall our last hug, both of us in tears, just outside an art store in Shahpur Jat close to his home. None of us cared who was around then, an irony in itself.

Christopher was just twenty-eight years old then. And unlike a Sukhdeep or an Anwesh or a Harsh or several others who were fighting for liberation and were quite free about who they were, he existed in a time warp that had caged him, keeping him away from a life he deserved that I wished he could have had and we could have shared.

Chapter Forty-six

SO, THERE I was with one more broken relationship. I was not sure if I would fall in love again or even wish to make an effort to meet new people. I feared slipping back into the deeper times of depression, something that Chitra repeatedly warned me of, trying to distract me with all kinds of discussions and outings, hoping I would regain a sense of balance.

I wrote several incomplete poems on sadness, loneliness and Christopher. There was only one that talked about a revival and that I would be back, implying I was not giving up just yet.

I travelled out of Delhi, not to Thailand but to Pune, Khapoli and Mumbai, trying to get some time on my own and away from the attractions and freedom that a Bangkok or a Phuket offered—all of which I had grown to realize, were momentary thrills, physical and commercial. I needed someone but I think I needed myself in full strength more than anyone else.

I even spent 31 December alone, entering the New Year lying in bed in a Pune hotel room. I had strolled in and out of malls in that city and spent hours walking through gardens and sitting on pavements pondering over nothing, watching people cross streets and cars go by.

It was not until I reached Mumbai and walked down Juhu beach that I felt a little revived, meeting old friends, analysing failed relationships and even loneliness—that dark side of life that my friends and I tried to throw light on! There were all kinds of theories—'move in with someone you like immediately' 'create a private space that is yours'. 'You can at least have a home,' was one such solution. 'Don't date someone who isn't out, there is too much baggage, duality,' was another suggestion. 'Be a sugar daddy, looking after your partner,' quipped another.

We all agreed it took two to tango but 'where the hell is that place for us to dance!' Or as someone said, 'Remain private, a life within a home and nothing more, nothing social,' an isolation of sorts, and if that is not possible, 'stay in touch over the phone, meet over weekends and take holidays' and live 'half an existence'.

While we were not sure what could change life for us, even an amended law, we all felt things had to get better. As a community, we were all hopeful that the judgement on privacy, in August of the previous year, was an indication of things to come. I remember Christopher and I were sitting having coffee in Bangkok when the order came in. We discussed the prospects of Section 377 being read down and chatted about civil rights including same-sex marriage and it being a reality much before any of us could have imagined.

While the media was sounding consistently supportive on the reading down of Section 377, on ground the debate had moved a lot forward. The idea of gender was slowly getting dismantled with intellectuals to youngsters challenging specific definitions as given by society or parents, breaking sexuality down into different identities. For people like me, this was a new debate, learning the several terms of CIS gender, intersex, and so on. There were individuals who refused to be labelled, some questioned the gender they were assigned at birth and others claimed it was best to remain fluid, knocking binaries out of the picture.

Their knowledge was a kind of confidence, shining beautifully. So much so, those friends who had once questioned my attraction for the younger lot were now singing a different tune. If you like them younger, there is nothing wrong with that, 'this is a generation to spend time with', I was told by a friend back in London, saying even a 25-year-old could be quite up there in terms of emotional maturity and awareness. And since I had started out when I was around thirty years old, that kind of placed me at par.

As I put myself together after Christopher, I felt that finding love may just be a pointless exercise; I hoped it would find me. At times, I had this strong feeling to remain single, have multiple lovers—friends with benefits—travel the world and leave everything to chance. But then again, I didn't wish to give up. Maybe a musician or a singer would come my way. Maybe, as I once wrote referring to what Ma had said, have more get-togethers at home, who knows, one of the men may stick around and not go away.

I had strange ideas of romance. I remember telling Christopher that we could go around the country as the gay duo doing acoustic sets at bars and cafes. I also dreamt of a cafe run by us, engaging with different people but hopefully most of them from our world—LGBTQ. Another thought was moving to Manipur, buying a patch of land and building something there.

While these thoughts slipped in and out of my head, the need to have someone did not die down, not even if I claimed I was fine and ready to move on. I called other friends, some who I had found attractive and some who had shown interest in me. I called Ahmed who was working with a publishing house. He was taken and was talking proudly about his love whom he had met in Bangkok. He had grown into a stronger, confident person, none of which was visible when we had met first. He was out at his workplace, not troubled as such, far younger than me, and 'living in a better time' as he had said once.

I also reached out to Ashwin, another Manipuri, but he was living in another country with his partner, a Frenchman. More calls and more disappointments followed. I had missed so many opportunities, I guess.

Chapter Forty-seven

IN A FEW months I was to turn fifty—a milestone not greater than the passage of time and the experiences I had had. Sometimes I wondered whether I'd be gone like Duji, a few months after fifty or like Pa who passed away when he was fifty-three.

Or did I, as many said, have a lot more of Ma in me, which meant carrying on till much past seventy, becoming a stronger person with every passing day. But a longer life was not something I was seeking.

There were occasions that Adi and I discussed living in the same building assuming we would both be single. I even heard that a group of queer people were buying land somewhere in Kerala, in an obscure part, planning to settle down there, far off from the 'typical' urban surroundings.

Even I had such thoughts, more often now than before. Living somewhere in Thailand or Luang Prabang in Laos—starting life over, in a charming anonymous way, more peaceful and less confined. But such thoughts were to be acted upon later, if I ever did. For now, we were awaiting for the order from the Apex Court, meeting and discussing the progress so far.

We were optimistic! Activists such as Maya Sharma based in Vadodara, who had been working for over forty years in this area, felt the reading down of Section 377 would allow a lot more advocacy and health work. Anjali had said that we could heave a sigh of relief if things went our way and focus on other rights. For many closeted, it would be a time to come out and say they are legal.

I wasn't sure what emotions were running through me. I wanted to stand up and say something hateful and abusive—maybe just a few words to get even with the jail of the normative I had lived in. It was strange, this feeling, but when I spoke to my old group of friends, the ones I used to hang out with back in 1999–2000, none of them cared much what the order would do or say.

Ironically, most of them were either single or were married to women and living outside the country in a civil union with another guy. Others were lost to death, having committed suicide or been killed by family members, murders that were hushed up.

Subhashish, the architect and blogger, an old friend I made at the Humrahi meetings, pointed out why we were where we were. 'Many of us spent a larger part of our lives gathering courage to be ourselves,' he said, implying there was very little energy or time left to connect with the opportunities of love. In any case, how many people were out for us to easily locate and date? How many felt safe to invest in a relationship or walk around, literally, in gay abandon.

As Subhashish put it, over the past few years, many were growing up 'being normal', finding themselves early and finding others as partners in their schools, colleges and workplaces, the way it was for heterosexuals. We had lost time, years of childhood to adulthood to our most productive working years, and now were probably set in our ways, not sure how much space we had left to accommodate another person or relationship.

It was only Justice Indu Malhotra—one of the judges who had collectively read down Section 377 on 6 September 2018, who realized our loss. 'History owes an apology to the members of this community,' she said, underlining a consciousness that we were compelled to live a life full of fear of reprisal and persecution.

Even she knew, I assume, that justice delayed was justice denied, a painful fact that I felt parents, society and media at large should have known long before. The order, obviously, was bound to change the paradigm, some of which was on display outside the court in full public view with a large representation of the community being themselves.

I was away with my family in Thailand to celebrate my fiftieth birthday, getting updates by the minute. Before we left, Ma had come to my room, teary-eyed, wondering if she had ever come in the way of anyone I had loved or wanted as a partner. She put out multiple choices—moving to another city or country, moving out to a separate space to start with or even to do the normal—insert a classified advertisement in one of the mainline papers.

'I don't want to carry any guilt with me,' she said, speaking like a loving mother who wanted to see her son settled. She herself had been through a journey, just as I had, learning that normal had many variants.

Even Uma masi told me years later that her first reaction was that of an uninformed person who loved me then and loves me a lot more now. She pushed me to adopt a child saying, 'Maybe the man of your life also wants to be a father, and will find you!'

Rita mami on the night of my fiftieth also said that she wanted to see me settled. 'Find someone of your level,' a point echoed by Ma, Sudhir uncle, Dilip and Nitin, who were also there. She even proposed Adi and wondered why he and I weren't together, not knowing we were never ever each other's 'type' and both of us were pretty much 'tops' in bed, which meant we would need a third person, if we ever considered living together!

My fiftieth was a normal celebration with normal conversations, leaving the final call entirely to me, even if I were to leave Delhi or the country. 'We would come and visit you all the time, wherever you are,' Dilip said, speaking for everyone at the table that night.

Chapter Forty-eight

AT FIFTY, I feel optimistic, exhausted, tired, not entirely out of depression, living with contradictions that swing from hope to despair.

On my return to Delhi, at a party held at home, a mix of friends—queer, activists, allies and musicians—celebrated the reading down of Section 377, raising a toast to those who had worked for us for so many years. The questions that did the rounds were: When will we get common space in society other than the confines of gay clubs, NGOs and private parties where we can be ourselves and find 'our' kind easily? Where are those streets where we can walk freely with the person we want to be with, without being judged? When will 'conversion' therapy be banned? When will society at large accept that homosexuality isn't a disease and their phobias need a cure? Will workplaces change their policies and become truly inclusive? And will cinema—the large influencer—have gay characters rather than caricatures? As I rummaged through various news reports and online features, I could see the word 'love' being used freely as though the court gave us the right to love and explore love fully. It was amazing how something as fundamental and basic as our rights was turned into a matter of affection and love when the emotions we went through were related to freedom to have sex and not to be criminalized for something as natural as that.

The normative and the conditioning of minds were so strong that the idea of sex was not about intimacy, lust or a need but about a construct called love and marriage. No wonder, the narratives that followed were about same-sex marriage—which is literally a personal choice—rather than civil rights, equal for everyone whether single or hitched in a union—polygamous or monogamous.

In a sense, we were seeking equity and were against discrimination of all kinds.

On TV, earlier on the night of 6 September, several activists on a debate that I was a part of through Skype, had argued that we needed civil rights and even a law that allowed civil unions equal to any marriage act. We needed to address issues of healthcare, insurance and inheritance and co-existence in schools to workplaces. In a way, it was made clear that no single person should be treated any less than a married individual, emphasizing that civil rights should not revolve around marriage alone.

Anjali and I sat one evening discussing all of this and more. She felt the years gone by have made me stronger but had also led me to lose faith in relationships, possibly closing the door on people who may have wanted to love me. 'This happens with the journey you have been through and the times we have lived in. While things will not change overnight or in a long time, you can't go away from the fight, nor can you close the door on love. Just open yourself once again, let love in, it will find a way,' Anjali told me as I left her home after our long discussion on why we need to still fight for equal rights and why each one of us had to be loved.

I, of course, couldn't be so despondent when many others had a life far worse than mine or similar.

If there was hope it lay in how the queer movement unified, even if polarized by the politics of the day. It lay in the new voices and courage. It resided in a changing media, more open and less biased. It was visible in earnest corporate leaders who genuinely wished to change their work culture and where we were not a part of a CSR programme. It lay in the history built over the years by the activists and lawyers who had fought collectively and independently.

For me, it was all of this and the acceptance and participation of friends and family in my life and the lives of others I had acquainted myself with. Even at the half-century mark—an age that seems kind of old—I turn to a precious message sent on my birthday by Chitra, the person who has known me so well: 'Seems strange to associate that number with you, for you have managed to hold on to a certain innocence and kindness that one usually associates with someone young, who has not gone through life yet. Best thing, your core is intact despite all the ups and downs.'

I was flattered and shared her message with many people in an act of self-indulgence. But I am certain and aware that there are many people out there, just like me, holding on to what Chitra says is a youthfulness that 'has not gone through life yet' defining my generation of queer people, particularly those who are still on the lookout for love.

Today, many of us are most likely disillusioned and reluctant, yet hopeful. Hopefulness, after all, had given us strength, making us see the brighter side life, allowing us laughs and joy to overcome and put a veil on our pain. We turned negative connotations such as fag and queer into positive terms and never once saw ourselves as skeletons in the closet—the nineteenth century term ascribed to coming out—as those who managed to 'come out' even if scarred, did so in full form, flesh and blood and not just bones. The movement can only get stronger. It can only get bigger, more vibrant, vocal and diverse. At every stage, like in the past, we seek only what is rightfully ours irrespective of whether our normalcy and sense of love will ever be 'straight' enough for society to grasp.

◆

The idea of what is normal
The idea of what is fate
The idea of what you are seeking
And the idea of mistakes

I was born to be a person
I was born to be who I am
You were born with the same story
That I am different is not a crime

The idea of what is nature
The idea of what's a freak
The idea of the difference
The distinctions are oblique

You were born to be normal
You do have some flaws
But who am I to intervene
And claim to cure you of what you are

The idea of the green leaves
The idea of the blue skies
The idea of night's darkness
The idea of daylight

They were born to be that way
They were born with their say
They were born to be different
No matter what you say

So if I am different, and if I am gay
And you are heterosexual
I am not curing you
Of your ways anyway

The idea that I am normal
The idea that I am gay
The truth is that we are different
And nature has had its say[1]

---

[1] The poem 'Nature Has Had Its Say' was written in January 2015 soon after a Goa government minister said he was setting up LGBT 'cure' centres.

Acknowledgements

Putting this book together has not been the easiest task. I had once penned down some 4,000 words in anger over a decade ago but never took it forward. I also attempted a fictionalized story with my friend, Rumy M. Narayan. But turning truth and facts into fiction was somehow not my cup of tea.

It was not until I met the hugely supportive Dibakar Ghosh at Rupa Publications India that the ball started to roll. He engaged with me almost every day, helping me meet what was a short submission deadline.

This book, however, would never have happened had it not been for so many people who have been a constant support to me in life and in writing my story. They include especially my uncles and aunts: Uma Malhotra, Rita and Sudhir Kapoor. Even my cousins on both sides of the family, across India, UK and the US have egged me on.

M.K. Venu and Chitra have helped in detailing some sections, making the story as real as possible. Even my friend Rohit Sharma would hear me out to see if I made sense, making suggestions from time to time. And then there is my childhood friend Nitin and his wife, Rachna, who kept my mood high and happy, allowing me to refer to awkward situations that we had experienced together.

Adhish Mehrotra, who saw me through some of the roughest periods of my life, helped ensure my memory was correct enough, laughing as we recollected some incidences from our past. I also had the support of Sujay Mehdudia who time and again got me to stay focused on the book.

I have also had candid narrations from my sister-in-law, Sonu Rangnekar, adding wealth to my story. Even Peggy Froerer—a person dear to our family—filled me in with conversations that I had only an inkling of.

There are undoubtedly so many more people who care and have touched my heart from time to time. Some of them are from my childhood in Mumbai, Kolkata and Delhi. Others are from my workplace, particularly *The Pioneer*, *The Economic Times* and Integral PR. I also had supportive members and partners from associations such as the PRCAI and PROI. I found allies who saw me through rough times specially those who associated with my band—Friends of Linger and the platform that I curated—Embrace: Music Justice Arts.

Above all of them has been my mother—Veena Rangnekar—and the kindest brothers one could have—my eldest brother, Dilip and the middle one, the late Dwijen Rangnekar.

My family loves who we are individually and together as a unit, is what frees me enough to bare my life in this book.

Thank you.